No, this book will not change your life. You have to do that. Like Ann Simons did. After her Olympic medal at the Olympic Games in Sydney in 2000, the judoka started the fight for her life. Without clear opponents, without applause, without podium. To become someone in the business world, where they are not welcoming athletes with open arm.

This book wishes to be a guide in discovering who you are, why you do what you do, how to realize your dreams. The search is often more important than the answer. The path to purpose.

THE PATH TO PURPOSE

Walking the path is more important than winning
ANN SIMONS

Content

GREEN BELT – Take charge
Pitfalls for the entrepreneurial leader

WELCOME TO LES ONDES
On a journey to yourself
FREE FROM YOURSELF

Supportive leadership in three belts
The base
BLUE BELT - Do not have expectations
BROWN BELT - Create the frame
BLACK BELT - Plant the seed

Pitfalls for the Supportive Leader

ON THE ROAD TOGETHER
Inclusive leadership: the seven belts in balance
Engaging
The path to purpose as an art of living
Including on exploration
Small is great
Sustainable goals
Ecosystem without egos
As a result
The guide in you

To tomorrowland

Introduction

Walking the path is more important than winning

What does a judoka have to do with inclusive leadership? Twenty years ago, Ann Simons exceeded all expectations as she won bronze at the Olympic Games. Today, she coaches young people to transcend themselves at the Cronos Group. Twenty years and five Olympic Games later, she looks back for the first time on her performance in Sydney in 2000. She describes the match day, analyses her matches and draws clear lessons from it.

Over the years, she developed 'the path to purpose', an art of living that connects entrepreneurial and supportive leadership in an inclusive model. An entrepreneurial leader takes responsibility for creating from within, in collaboration with others. For a supportive leader, the ultimate challenge is to break free from themself to empower someone else, without expecting direct recognition.

Simons makes the links between her experiences as an Olympian and as a coach of young entrepreneurs. Sometimes growing slowly, away from the spotlight, often starting from their inner strength, independent but in solidarity, each at his or her own pace. Modern entrepreneurial stories.

Using the seven colored belts we know from judo, she builds a system that transcends systems thinking. A structure which is anything except rigid, but fluid, a process that lives and grows. At the end point, which is just as much a starting point, the seven belts merge in a cycle that allows to switch freely between entrepreneurship and support. Back when necessary, forward when possible. The path to purpose.

As a leader, striving from within to make your own dream come true, while at the same time, as a leader, striving to make someone else fulfil his or her dream. You can place both angles on a spectrum, from extreme entrepreneurial leadership to extremely supportive leadership. The path to purpose takes you to the appropriate intersection, depending on the context and the needs of those involved. It is about the courage to keep moving, not to be pinned down, to constantly question where you are and why you are there.

The extremely entrepreneurial leaders interpret things based on their own agenda, they focus on winning and put their ego at the center. To them, people are a means to increase financial capital. Often, they make their dreams come true at the expense of the other.

The supportive leaders at the other end serve their environment at the expense of themselves. Often, they lose sight of the bigger picture because of this.

A balance is desirable. Interesting ideas emerge on both sides of the spectrum. *Conscience* can help us navigate between them.

Consciousness as a moral compass. A sense of justice and fairness.

A value set that transcends religion, culture, geography, nationality, and race.

Independent of the time and space in which we live.

"What's good for me?" But also: 'What is good for the other and what can I do for that?' The path to purpose is a constant pursuit of balance. A plea for desirable, human balance. An art of living. Hannah Arendt described it as follows: 'Without love and the shared responsibility

for the world - *Amor Mundi* - there is insufficient counterbalance offered to the *Amor Sui*, the selfishness, the ego that as the primacy of capitalism applies.'

An inclusive leader places a company at the heart of society.

Like an ecosystem without ego. Economically responsible and socially aware. What is good for one person must be good for another. Together on the path to purpose to tomorrow. Awareness is also growing on Wall Street that companies should not only provide added value for shareholders, but also for the interests of employees, customers and the serve wider community. Greed is gradually giving way to sustainability, diversity, and well-being. A company is not an island, but (one part of) an ecosystem.

The path to purpose is another way of dealing with the challenges of the twenty-first century: the continuous change, the uncertainty and complexity. In 2020 we are in the middle of the fourth industrial revolution. The boundaries between real and virtual, economy and ecology, life and work fade. Robotics, nanotechnology, the internet of things, Artificial Intelligence; developments are occurring faster and faster. How we produce, consume and interact with each other will change fundamentally.

With this book Ann Simons serves as our guide on the path to purpose, where walking the path is more important than winning, where people are more than competitors and where a follower can also become a leader. Positive and inclusive. Working together.

Lessons from judo
The soft cradle

We start with a bow. No, that is not a sign of submission, just a gesture of mutual respect. We both bow, writer and reader, and we lean towards each other. That is how we will close the book.

After which we each go our way. On a gentler path, by then.

But first, back in time, to where the sun rises. Judo has deep roots in Japanese history. More than a combat sport, it is the art of self-defense. The martial arts from which judo originated were a lot less gentle. At its origin is jiu-jitsu, a collective name for the techniques used by the samurai, who were masters. In 1882, Professor Jigoro Kano developed judo further. When he was barely 22, he opened his first judo school Tokyo, the kodokan. This dojo (rehearsal space) is still the sanctuary of judo sport.

Jigoro Kano did not agree with the rough techniques of the traditional jiu-jitsu and taijutsu that he had to master as a student. As a student of philosophy and pedagogy at the University of Tokyo he integrated mental aspects and manners in his new art of defense, in addition to physical training. Master Kano selected techniques to eliminate the opponent without seriously injuring him. It became the basis of judo.

The current competition variant differs greatly from the basic form such as Kano developed. The original premise was that strength would not play a meaningful role. By correctly applying the learned techniques, a small and weak person should be able to defend himself in an elegant way
against a large and strong attacker. Kano exhausted the rich Japanese combat traditions, but he omitted certain combinations of locking and throws from the repertoire. They can be dangerous if the partner does not sufficiently master the technique of rolling.
Originally judo was a self-defense art in which two concepts from the philosophy of Jigoro Kano are central.

Seiryoku-Zenyo
Maximum effectiveness with minimum effort
Whatever you do, it must be done with the best possible use of mental and physical energy. In judo we learn to use the power of the opponent to overthrow him. In daily life this translates into choosing the right actions at the right moment.

Jita-Kyoei
Mutual benefit and well-being
We, as judokas, should have respect for ourselves and for others. Only by working together can we learn skills. You are nothing without your opponent. You need someone who will fall for you and you have to fall for someone else. This view of collaborative learning is also applicable in other areas. We cannot move forward if we are not able to serve the other.

The path to purpose that I describe in this book strives for leadership based on these principles. Towards a new art of living without end. A cycle. An infinity, if you will. It is an interplay effectiveness and efficiency, doing the right things and not just doing the things right, and striving for sustainable wellbeing on the other. In there lies the art of living the path to purpose: always knowing how to find the balance between seemingly contradictory dilemmas.

Since childhood I have been passionate about judo and the philosophy around it.
After my professional sports career, the passion for competition judo, where power plays a much greater role, has faded away. My passion for judo has remained as an art of living. The measure of power has been exchanged for a measure of value. Participation is really more important than winning.

A lot of lines can be drawn between judo and leadership. With much respect for Jigoro Kano I want to bundle them together into a path. A few parallels:
• Judo and the path to purpose as an art of living are based on balance.
• Where competition judo revolves much more around the fight and the ego, the path to purpose is about *conscience*, consciousness,

conscience: the inner voice that connects us with who we really are. *Conscience* as a counterpart to ego.

• Both tackle dilemmas and defuse apparent contradictions.

• Sustainably looking forward. Jigoro Kano thought about how a small person could defend themselves against a bigger attacker, but in a sustainable way, without hurting him unnecessarily. On the path to purpose a leader sees the future before the other sees it. And he facilitates the other in a gentle way to believe in himself, so that the future is created in a sustainable way, instead of controlled.

• Letting go rather than controlling. Without going into detail about the techniques of judo, they work much better when we are relaxed, when we enjoy the game and get energy from it. Also, on the path to purpose of the inclusive leader, letting go and creating from there is preferred to controlling.

• The path to purpose has rights and obligations. I do not know of any sport in which discipline plays such a big role as it does in judo. Walking the path to purpose as an art of living also requires a lot of discipline and a deep understanding of it rights and obligations.

• We do it together. On the path to purpose, we are nothing without the other. It is a form of inclusive leadership. Only together with others can we achieve something. We exist because the other exists. We go forward because the other is willing to serve us.

I have chosen to build the path to purpose around colors, not coincidentally the successive belts in judo. The difference is that in judo they say something about the level of mastery, but in the path to purpose as an art of living that is not the case. Living according to the seven color belts can push humanity forward in a sustainable way, without losing sight of human well-being.

In the next chapter, I'll take you to the Olympics in Sydney, the highlight of my judo career. The importance of yourself and knowing others is a common thread through that day. You can see it too as a start and end point on the path to purpose as an art of living.

Olympic dreams

And waking up in Sydney

Have you worked so hard for this?
Are you letting the chance for Olympic glory pass?
Is that what you have to show the world?
Wake up!

Four short sentences. Eddy De Smedt did not need more. He was my *mental facilitator* at the Olympic Games in Sydney. It was 16 September 2000. The day it had to happen. The wake-up call worked. That day I would fight my best match ever. He made sure I did not get distracted by my emotions and the environment. The inner voices were silent. I could focus on my mission.

For many athletes, Eddy De Smedt, the elite sports director of the Belgian Olympic Interfederal Committee (BOIC), was a counselor. You could talk to him about anything. He was there always and everywhere, seemingly invisible. His gift: making others shine. Eddy empowered us. As a leader in the shadows, he understood the art of creating a tailor-made context.

I owe my bronze medal in Sydney to countering my own emotions. The most important lesson after ten years of judo at the very highest level: you can only reach the absolute world top if you do not let your feelings rule your life, when you have the courage to walk your own path, and take control of what you have built.

From that one day I learned that you make progress when you know both yourself and the other. Who are you and why are you doing it? What are your strengths and your weaknesses? What are your passions? What gives you energy? Where are the pitfalls and how do you avoid them? How do you keep emotions under control? How do you transcend the context to see the bigger picture? It is a story of skills and personality. It is what distinguishes supportive leadership from other forms of leadership.

In judo we speak of an opponent. In this book I'll talk about 'the other'. In 'real' life, the other does not have to be an opponent or competitor. Just like you want to find out who you are, you have to be curious about her or him. Only then can success be sustainable.

Olympic Dreams

16 September 2000

The Sydney Olympic Games. 'My' Games. I have worked for this for so long. As soon as I get up, I feel it: this will be my day.

It is Sacha, as we call national coach Alexander Jatskevitch, who wakes me. Together we cycle through the Olympic village on the way to the first hurdle: the official weigh-in.

At every tournament, judokas are weighed at 7 in the morning. Child's play. However? Not for me. My entire career has been a fight for to dive under those 48 kilograms (the lightest weight class at the women). Ten grams too much and you are immediately disqualified. Done before it even started. It took me months of dieting to get here. Sometimes no more than two yogurts, one apple and two slices of chicken breast for six hours of training. It is not just a physical fight but above all a mental battle – it rules your entire life. I spent more time making my weight than visualizing the competition.

If you weigh one or two kilograms too much the evening, it will be misery. 'Fluid training', as it is called in the jargon. Imagine it is 26 degrees in the torture of a musty eastern European hotel and you need to still put on a sweat suit. It is a refined garbage bag, a straitjacket made of plastic in which your body instantly goes red. As if you were training in a pressure cooker. You run from one side to the other, one hour, one and a half hours, two hours if you have to, until you hit the walls. Then one warm bath, not always in the most hygienic conditions. Then in bed under a thick blanket, overheated, dehydrated, dizzy, nauseated. You do not know what you should be feeling, you just know that you are sweating.

After a cool shower, you step on the scale: between 47 and 47.5 kilogram - in my case usually anyway. That means I have lost three kilograms fluid or more than five percent of my body weight. I can drink and (to a lesser extent) eat until I weigh 48.4. The experience has taught

me that I will still lose a minimum that night, even after three kilograms of dehydration. Apparently, it is part of the judo world: everyone trains down, suffers. It is not just your fat that goes, but also way too much moisture. I have had blocked kidneys or a bladder infection several times.
Until today I have to be aware of it.

It is not easy to fall asleep the day before a match. A cocktail of stress and thirst and once asleep, the same dreams, or better, nightmares: either my mouth is gagged so that I can never drink anything again, or I crawl on all fours through one huge drinks hall, from palette to palette, opening a bottle every time but barely being allowed to sip. I wake up, fearing that I drank too much. The only advantage: cold sweat is also less moisture.

For Sydney, I balanced my weight so well that I only had to lose one kilogram while there. A world of difference. At supper time I weigh 47.3 kilograms, so I am allowed to drink and even eat some pasta. That evening it is quiet in the dining room at the Olympic Village. Most athletes, counselors and coaches have left for the opening ceremony. I let it pass me by, tomorrow is the match.

The cyclists also compete on the first day of the Games. We eat a light meal together. I am sitting next to Axel Merckx. He tells me what he expects from his first Games. Later, he will discuss the tactics for tomorrow with his father Eddy, the greatest of all. I feel the magic of be able to be part of this family. These are the Olympics. You feel it in every fiber of your toned body, in every pumped heartbeat. Competitions, opponents, preparation, focus: in principle everything is the same. And yet everything is different.

After dinner I stroll through the village for a while, seeing some of the opening ceremony on the screens. Peace and stability. When I look back later, I realize that these are crucial factors, the basis for sustainable success. That morning, I am very relaxed. I slept well. On the way on the bike I meet a group of Dutch athletes. I am early, still have some time and have a chat with some judokas I know from the preparation. We often sit together with the Dutch on training camps abroad.

Pieter van den Hoogenband is also there, very relaxed. The Dutch swimmer will become Olympic champion in the 100 meters freestyle that week. 'A weigh-in?' He asks. They do not know that concept in his sport. I explain it to him and notice that I am getting a little nervous. To the scales.

The verdict: 47.5 kilograms. Damn, I still could have had a can of Fanta last night. But I feel good, so no problem. Near fainting is not an issue, and no other inconveniences that can arise if you have eaten or drunk too little. That does not alter the fact that I immediately take two bottles of Aquarius and a liter of water when I go out. The rice cake tastes so good that my eyes sparkle - I think about my son now, when he gets not one but two scoops of ice cream.

With Sacha I cycle to the large dining room in the Olympic village. After the months-long diet nightmare I now end up in a dream: a breakfast buffet for ten thousand athletes and coaches, of all cultures, for every allergy, cold and warm, healthy and fat. Would you like a hamburger in the morning? It is possible. I do not know what to choose. So, pasta without sauce with brown sugar. Such as for every match. The croissants, cookies filled with white cream and *pancakes* with blueberries I ignore. Maybe tomorrow if I fight well today.

After all, this is the day around which an entire sports career revolves, the most important
of my life as a top athlete. The plate of pasta with brown sugar tastes great and I have not died of thirst. Together with Sacha I watch the draw. It always takes place the night before the tournament starts. Some judokas insist on seeing it before going to sleep. Not me.
Drink slowly first. In retrospect, I realize that I just have to resign myself to certain circumstances. You just have to deal with some things. A bad or good draw, it is what it is. The draw is your fate. It can always be worse. In my first match I meet an unknown Tunisian

judoka. Should be feasible.

Due to the time difference with the rest of the world, the matches start in Sydney at 1 pm. I still have some time. In the Olympic village the togetherness is almost tangible. Preparing for camp here is very different from lying on your bed in a hotel in the former Eastern Bloc where the elevator only works for an hour a day. Sometimes those are the circumstances too.

I will forever remember the ride through the Olympic village after breakfast. It gives me a peace of mind that I never felt again in my sports career. For a moment I manage to escape the focus of day. I have been in a flow all morning. A flow that is not blurry, the details are razor-sharp. And they have stayed that way.

A red van takes me to the judo temple. After that it apparently goes on to the tennis courts, because by chance I end up on the seat next to Lleyton Hewitt, then-fiancé of Kim Clijsters. The Australian is on his way to his first singles match. Normally I am not approachable before a competition, but my curiosity prevails. Lleyton regrets that Kim is not there. If they get married soon, he says laughing, they might be able to compete in the mixed doubles together at the next Olympic Games. It is not meant to be.

I am among the first in the hall. My father and my club coach are already there. Intuitively I step onto the mat - today the ladies in the 48 kilograms category will complete their program here. I am a lady and I weigh less than 48 kilograms. This is my mat. Since no one is here yet, I do my stretching here. I breathe in the atmosphere, absorb the moment. In this magnificent hall there are only two tatamis, one for the women and one for the men. There are two weight categories on the schedule each day, split evenly. Today it is the turn for the lightest female and male judokas. The tournament will be completed in one day for everyone. If you go to the end, you may have to fight seven times.

For me, the whole day revolves around the experience and the magic of the moment.

After stretching in the competition hall, I continue to warm up in an adjacent space that is only accessible to athletes. I am excited without being stressed. I am ready. Then my name blares through the speakers. It is time. It is about time.

We start with 23 judokas. We had to all qualify on our own continent. The battle beforehand was long and been tough. In my case mainly a mental battle against Ilse Heylen. Ilse had come into my category to have a chance to participate in the Games. In Europe she was my biggest competitor. The first five of the European rankings are guaranteed an Olympic ticket, with a limit of one judoka per country per weight category. In April 2000, Ilse and I were ranked first and second respectively on the European qualification list ahead of the last qualifying tournament in Rotterdam. If Ilse won gold, she would go and I couldn't. Of course, we met in the final - a screenwriter couldn't have come up with it. Regardless of our previous performances, everything was decided in Rotterdam. Whoever won could go to her first Olympic Games. That's how hard sport can be.

Barely four months later, an eternity it seems, I am standing here in Sydney to face a Tunisian girl. I do not know her. Early in the game I take the lead. But then the engine starts to sputter. The stress screeches through my body. I'm starting to doubt myself - who am I actually fighting? Against an unknown Tunisian or against one side of myself that I do not know? The fear is paralyzing. I have lost my focus. I reach the end. I win. Do not ask me how.

An Australian presents herself in the second camp. The host country will end up with medals in many sports, but judo is not immediately their field. I also do not know this judoka. It will not be a top match, but I do what I need to do. Less than half an hour later, the quarter-final follows, against the German Anna-Maria Gradante. Throughout the judo world she is the one I get along with best. She is also one of the few judokas who is fluent in English. Nine months before Sydney, she was in a car accident, her preparation was therefore far from optimal.

Once on the mat my head fills with voices. I should not have been so kind to her, even though she was almost a friend. She did not have to take that hard road to qualify. Anna-Maria had already qualified through the world championship one year before the Games.
I have lost my focus and that in the most important match of my life. Why am I doing things that do not matter at the time?! The match ends scoreless. The three referees must appoint a winner. One of them thinks I deserve to go to the semi-finals. That is one too few. I am referred to the retakes.

Looking back, I realize that in this game the foundation was laid for my transition to supportive leadership. A supportive leader knows the other and him or herself. This is the only way to make success about more than just winning. It is the beginning of durability.

Do not know yourself and do not know the opponent
and you have hardly any chance of winning.
Know yourself, but not the opponent

and you have a 50 percent chance of winning.
Do not know yourself, but the adversary does,
and you have a 50 percent chance of winning.
Know yourself and the opponent,
and you have the greatest possible chance of
winning.
(The Art of War)

In the fight against Anna-Maria, I was not concerned with myself, nor was I with her. I specifically wanted to 'not lose', but you will never win that way. I do not want to continue after the loss. I cannot do get gold anymore anyway. I criticize myself in front of others. I take off my kimono and exchange it for my tracksuit.

Enter Eddy De Smedt, the elite sports director of the BOIC and the personification of calm.
Loved by every athlete. He can give you the confidence to go the *extra mile*. I started working with Eddy six months before. He was there for me when I felt like I was all alone. He helped me understand the jumble of emotions: through fatigue, homesickness, frustration.

When I did not feel like have another four-hour workout, which means as much as four hours of pain. I am sitting on a table, in my tracksuit. My kimono in front of me, ready to never be worn again. Two heaps of misery. And then Eddy speaks these four sentences:

Have you worked so hard for this?
Will you miss the chance for Olympic glory?
Is that what you have to show the world?
Wake up!

The fighting spirit is back in a flash. I want to fight for bronze. With every fiber in my body, every newly tensed nerve.

In the first round of the elimination, a Mexican judoka awaits me. A young fighter. Think: exotic beach full of boys playing football and one girl in shorts and bikini, her long black hair tied together, shoulders and hips the same width. But I believe in myself. And I have trained with her, I know her. These will be my Olympics again. The emotions can go back into the trunk of the bus for a while. I win.

In the next round I meet Amarilis Savón. After Anna-Maria Gradante, this is the second key fight of the day. This is going to be very tough. Savón is a Cuban top judoka who I have never been able to beat. In fact, I have never completed a fight with her. She always scores with ippon. Regulations then determine that the regular time will no longer be completed. Like a knockout in boxing. Today she has very unexpectedly lost a match, so she ended up in the elimination round.

With my club coach Jean-Jacques - he sits next to my father in the hall - I have practiced for hours on Savón's weak spots. She does not have many. Jean-Jacques acted as a dummy to reenact Savón. While those endless sessions we searched for the key to defeat her. Every time again from another position, anticipating all her movements. We spent days in the judo hall in Lommel, full of thoughts and frustrations, but also with little pieces of progress.

The match starts well, within thirty seconds I gain half a point, the second highest score. If you score two half points, it is also game over. There are still three and a half minutes left on my clock to defend my lead. Fear strikes me again. What now? What do I have to do? I cannot keep this, she's going to beat me. From the grandstand, Jean-Jacques shouts: "The second option!" I do what we understand by that and score again. A lower score, yes, but the coast is one again slightly safer.

I constantly focus on both my and her strengths and weaknesses, am not concerned with the consequences of the contest - win or lose. That is how I create the peace to control myself and thus the fight. It almost goes without saying. I am over the moon. Later that week I run into Savón in the athletics stadium. She tells me she felt an inconceivable strength in me. That I was completely in the game and would not let her use her usual tactics. That I got her out of her rhythm so much that she could only focus on me, could not fight on her own, let alone her strengths.

It is one of the best compliments I have ever received on my judo. I executed my own strategy to perfection and did not ask myself the question whether I would win or lose. My focus was on the path, playing with decisions based on the circumstances that arise at that moment. The path to purpose.

'Know yourself and the opponent and you have the greatest possible chance to win.' I had succeeded in putting the principle into practice.

Last call. I am almost immediately summoned to my last camp, the one for bronze. I just turned 20, I am in my second year at the University of Brussels. These are my first Games and I get to fight for an Olympic medal. The adrenaline. I just beat my role model and now I am up against Cha Hyon-Hyang from North Korea. I do not know her at all. You never see North Koreans at other international competitions, but they come incognito to film their opponents. This way they can study it, analyze it and devise strategies. My strength from the previous fight, namely that I knew Savón through and through and could respond to every change was now my weakness.

'Know yourself, but not the opponent, and you have a 50 percent chance of to win.' Cha knows exactly who I am. All I know is that she narrowly lost the semi-final to Ryoko Tamura, the five-time world and Olympic champion. Maybe even unfairly.

The contest starts very closed. My Korean opponent does not give an inch, I do not get a chance to carry out any of my favorite techniques. We both seem frozen. And then she scores anyway. Minimal, but she found an opening. She now sets the rhythm. She can anticipate every attempt by me to turn the tide. She dances effortlessly around me. I get frustrated, get penalized for passive judo because she knows perfectly how to block me. I am two small scores behind. I have to find a solution, break the pattern, take control of the fight. But it does not work. Five seconds to the end, the referee interrupts the game for the last time.

Suddenly I hear Jean-Marie Dedecker calling. Six months before the start of the Olympic Games he was fired by the Flemish Judo Federation and he is no longer allowed to coach us directly. But he can from the stands. 'Do it now, you can do it!' I instinctively know that I can do 'it'. From deep within myself I generate a final wave of attack. Which is so powerful that the North Korean falls over. I score. I win. I have Olympic bronze.

Of course, Cha has made a crucial mistake. With only five seconds left on the clock she just had to stay away from me. Use judo regulations and my panic to her advantage. Running away is punishable by a slight counter score, never enough for me to still be able to win. But overconfident and with the focus only on herself, she approached me. She was no longer aware of my strengths.

Whether you know yourself and your opponent or not, fall into the trap of overconfidence and you have no chance of winning. You start to make mistakes that always make you lose in the short or longer term. Also as a person. Overconfidence slows down your growth, stops progress. You forget to focus on yourself and the other. There is too much focus on the outcome and too little on the path. The North Korean made that mistake at a very important time in her sports career. And in mine.

On the way is the way
Done with the Games
This book is not a biography of my judo career, but my experiences in sports have left an indelible mark on it. How I look at social progress, what role I can play in it, how contrary that role sometimes is to my past life as a top athlete... The path to a meaningful existence is not always easy, on the contrary. Sometimes it seems impenetrable, it often goes fast, or it is playing hardball.

Still, I stuck to the title, 'the path to purpose'. It is the literal translation of 'judo' from Japanese, and above all it expresses my hope to contribute towards a softer future, inclusive and with solidarity. Where to participate and doing business is more important than winning. I invite the reader to also look at progress in relation to personal well-being, rather than from a purely economic point of view. At the moment, I give substance to that myself by building Wingmen, an incubator for young people who want to do business based on their passion, in mental and financial safety, and who put well-being and self-realization above financial gain.

Both my experiences in top sport and those with young entrepreneurs were a source of inspiration when writing. I wish to share my view on inclusive leadership. It is a work ethic and an art of living that invites the leaders of tomorrow to reflect on their position and their responsibility. It challenges us to choose between dilemmas, depending on what it takes. The philosophy of judo is the central thread throughout. On the face of it my adventure in Sydney
and forward-looking, inclusive leadership, are not so much related. But that day can illustrate both the starting and the end point of the path to purpose. Knowing yourself and the other as the alpha and the omega.

By losing sight of that inseparable duality, I lost a crucial game during the Olympics. When I regained consciousness - figuratively - I could start from within again and take into account the strengths and weaknesses of the other. And that is how I won the two most important camps of my sports career.

Until I was 26, I only knew one world and that was that the world of sports. Although I traveled halfway around the world and experienced other cultures, when I entered the job market, I felt out of touch. It is said that as a former top athlete you have a number of qualities that others can only dream of. That's right, otherwise you'd never made it to the top. It is also a great happiness to work on yourself like that. It made me the person I am today. I still breathe sports.

But elite sports also closes off paths and blows up bridges. It won't allow you to build an identity separate from your ego. You become your outside. Once outside that 'world' you are therefore stuck with a huge disadvantage. In elite sports, everything revolves around you. Your whole environment will conform to that self-centeredness. You are the center of attention. Without that mindset, you won't put in a world-class performance - in any career.

After a career switch, you tumble off the stage. The Olympian has to go back to school. In the entry-level class you are one of many. The ego collapses like quickly (or badly) built Lego. What after sports? I never really wanted or could think about it. My study choice was more in function of my judo career rather than out of a passion for economy. This only made the lag in the labor market more poignant. Nobody is welcoming you with open arms.

At first you feel deprived of yourself, of your opportunities, but gradually you see the enrichment. You meet many people looking for a job. Often people who look at the world completely differently, and do not necessarily have anything to do with sport. I had to find my place again between them.

My big dream, for which I had worked for fifteen years, had come true. Now I was startled. Who was I? What could I do? Where to start? Which direction? Why had I been doing judo for so long? Did I make the right choice? I looked around and I looked in the mirror. I thought I knew myself. It became a fight I was not trained for. Painful, but meaningful. I learned that leadership is a spectrum, a maze of dilemmas that you have to go through again and again. Just because of those different and extreme forms of leadership the world will end up moving forward in the long term .

Life is a path, in all its infinity. For me who only lived on achieving goals and results, an entire mind shift.

People who change the world have a higher mission. They take strength from the belief that they are able to allow a group of people to look at things differently. Their *legacy* is that others can build on that. That their inheritance is not a will, but a statement of principles.

How to handle leadership in times of change? The journey also showed me that complexity, inefficiency and diversity should not be detrimental for the individual well-being. Thinking ahead sustainably leaves plenty of room for that. We live and work with people who think, speak and judge differently.

Similar thinking limits people and does not contribute to self-realization and thus also not to well-being. Compare it to a banana plantation, where the complexity, diversity and personal input are kept to a minimum. Everything runs according to standard procedures and that generates money. While the jungle around is buzzing with complexity and diversity, although without efficiency.

The path to purpose shows you the forest through the trees. It leads to self-realization. Participation and entrepreneurship are more important than winning and acquiring. The path is the way.

From within yourself
Enterpreneurial leadership in four belts

The base

Realizing your own dream
Together with a team
Selling your creations
Delivering to everyone's satisfaction

An enterpreneurial leader is based on these four pillars. He is the center of his company or organization, in between his team and his customers. Everything starts from his dream. From there he starts creating. But dreams remain dreams if you do not attach goals to them. To achieve them, it is best to divide a dream into milestones. You can then work towards it with your team. Abstract becomes concrete.

An entrepreneur is also busy selling his creations or products and delivering them in such a way that the customer is satisfied. Customer satisfaction is indispensable for the entrepreneurial leader. Fed by his team and his customers, the entrepreneurial leader can take a step forward.

Dream, go for it and work on it together. Entrepreneurial leadership summed up in a few simple words. They were spoken by Olivier Daenen, the 27-year-old owner and entrepreneurial leader of Entrepot del Tartufo, an Italian restaurant in Hasselt where I regularly went for lunch with my friend Wim while writing this book.

Together with a team. In this twenty-first century the principles of leadership are fundamentally called into question. Top-down collaboration becomes open and flexible. The challenges facing organizations are complex and capricious: accelerating technological development,
increasing regulation and control, increasingly social commitment and awareness of the ecological footprint.

As an entrepreneurial leader you also know how to develop relationships and bring knowledge together by listening and asking questions. You learn and connect. Which requires a vulnerable position. You have to dare to admit that you do not know everything. The relationship and not the position determines the result. Leading successfully in times of change is done through shared goals and ambitions, focused on personal, social and ecological sustainability. Like Robert Greenleaf, the founding father of servant leadership, stated: 'People rise above themselves when those who lead them, understand them and accept them as they are, even if their performance is critically assessed on the basis of their abilities. '

If you want to create from within yourself, together with others, without crossing someone else's limits, it is essential that they have confidence in you as an entrepreneurial leader. Once that is the case, the chances increase of getting team members to follow the path you have mapped out.

An entrepreneurial leader ...
- starts from his own dream.
- chooses who he wants to work with.
- is open to opportunities.
- takes control and continues the journey, even in the event of a setback.
- creates added value together with a team. He ensures that every member matters. This is often translated financially. Which can also be a pitfall as discussed later in this book.
- is visible. He is applauded when he succeeds and is dismissed when results are poor.
- shows the courage to lead the way. He dares to make decisions that go against the norm.
- is forgiving. He allows people to make mistakes and get angry with him.
- is a good storyteller. He knows how to include people in his story.
- allows his employees their own momentum. An entrepreneurial leader does not see team members merely as resources. He gives them opportunities, just as he got himself.

The four belts. A few times a year I travel with a group of young, passionate people to Les Ondes, a safe haven of the Cronos Group in the Ardennes, for a *leadership journey* (more about that special place later in the book). They all have their own dream, all of them want to take the next step. How grateful I am to them. Because they dared to adopt a vulnerable position, beyond shame and allow me to experience unique moments with them.

Starting from who I am and from my own past, I got a sense of where they stand in life, and where they want to go. To everyone who recognizes this: congratulations! You also helped me take another step to write this book. You gave me the inspiration to capture the four belts of entrepreneurial leadership.

White Belt
Take responsibility
You alone are responsible for your life
Focus on what you can control
Consciously choose how you deal with the choice of someone else
Inspire your team to take responsibility
It makes you and them vulnerable and proud

As they grow up, children become more and more aware that they are responsible for their own lives. It is a learning process: what can you do yourself, when do you call for help? They become independent, physically, mentally, emotionally, spiritually and financially. Still there are many people today, men and women, who remain dependent on others just because they are not fully aware of the responsibility for their own lives. The situation they are in is a result of how they interact with events and encounters of the past. They blame the error, fault or cause of it on someone else.

Of course, the choices of others also affect you. But even if you bear the consequences, you have no part in that choice. When you take the take responsibility for your own life, you accept that someone else's choice does not have to be yours. You do decide how you deal with the consequences of that choice.

Someone who is not aware
of the responsibility for his or her own life
focuses on the choice of the other when something goes wrong;
is and remains dependent and gets frustrated.

Someone who is aware
of the responsibility for his or her own life
looks at what he / she can do to deal with the choice of the other;
becomes independent and confident.

It is a matter of choice: stand still or progress? "I did not choose that." A lot of people hide behind that sentence to explain their personal stagnation. While they themselves are to blame for not progressing and hindering their self-realization.

An example. A husband decides to divorce his wife. She can keep repeating that it is not her choice. A nasty divorce becomes inevitable, because as a woman you are trapped in the mindset that you are and will remain dependent on the choices of your future ex. A value conflict is imminent, because the husband wants to go on independently of his wife, but she does not accept his choice.

You can also choose a different way to deal with your partner's choice. Accept that the prospective ex has made a choice that was not yours, that it hurts, but that you take responsibility for what comes next. The cards are on the table, the situation is what it is.

Despite the suffering others may cause you, it is up to you to make the most of it. Taking responsibility for your own life means that you focus on the things you have control over. If a customer or someone on your team wants to leave, you can try to persuade him or her to stay, but the ultimate choice rests with him or her. It can be a hard message, a relationship - it can also be a work relationship - which is over, but you have to learn to accept that people around you make choices without you. How you deal with that, you have that decision in your hands. Do you get caught up in anger, frustration, confusion? Do you get stuck in something that you cannot do anything about, namely the choice of the other? Or do you look at yourself and the tools you have, refuse to let yourself be guided by the consequences and take the initiative?

Empower yourself. This is the only way to achieve true independence. And it is indispensable for an enterpreneurial leader who manages a team.

It is much easier to pass the blame or the shame on another. This also emerges during the *leadership* weekends in Les Ondes. Participants sigh that the situation they are in happened to them is - dismissal, illness, divorce... Indeed things you did not choose.

Taking responsibility for your own life requires vulnerability, strength and patience. It is the only way to self-realization, a choice between standing still and progress. Do you want to be a good entrepreneurial leader, then you cannot ignore the 'responsibility for your own life'. Without
that it is impossible to start from who you are and what you dream of, with a team to invent, create, sell and deliver.

An example. Marc Herremans showed great promise in triathlon. It was written in the stars that he would one day be the Ironman of Hawaii win, with 3.86 km swimming, 180.2 km cycling and 42.195 km running the toughest race in the world. On October 6, 2001, he finished sixth there.

And then disaster struck. After a fall during a cycling training in Lanzarote at the beginning of 2002 he became paralyzed and ended up in a wheelchair. For a top athlete like Marc, the nightmare can hardly be darker. Of course, he couldn't change the fact that he was paralyzed. However, he did everything he could to continue as a triathlete. With a custom-made bicycle and by swimming purely on arm strength, he competes in special triathlons. In 2003 Herremans finished the Ironman in Hawaii, from start to finish. On October 22, 2006 he was the first to cross the line.

He also started the organization To Walk Again, which conducts research to spinal cord injuries. He runs his own training center and is a coach to triathletes and other athletes. In the management of his team as an entrepreneurial leader, his employees feel he is giving 100 percent. They share his dream and trust him.

We have not always chosen what happens to us. We do not choose to get sick, we do not choose to get fired, we do not choose for our partner to divorce us, as a child we do not choose to have two homes after a divorce, we do not choose to have an accident. What we do choose is how we deal with it. How we respond to events that we must accept and cannot control.

Entrepreneurial leaders are convinced that the present is a consequence of the past, and that today's choices have an impact on the relationships of tomorrow. Giving your kids that mindset is one great gift. Thus, they learn to focus their energy on what they own and not to waste on things beyond their control.

Another example. During a *leadership journey* I saw that something was wrong with Jeroen. He only knew for a few days that Torben, the Norwegian with whom he would start a business had chosen to return to his homeland. He wanted to continue doing business together. Jeroen told me that he would no longer like that if Torben did not live in Belgium. Which felt like he had no real business partner. I explained to him that he did not affect Torben's decision to return to Norway, but he could choose how he saw the continuation, and with it write a story that was in line with his values and foundations. Look within himself and jump out of the box.

They gave it a chance: a remote company. Jeroen would bring a team together in Hasselt, Torben in Oslo, all around the same technology. Now, Torben has ten people under his wing. Jeroen, who moved as well, to the Netherlands, leads the Benelux team of thirty people. They skype with each other on a daily basis, and meet every two weeks, one time in Oslo, the other time in Amsterdam.

Every few months Jeroen comes for coffee. I enjoy those wonderful moments. As a passionate entrepreneur under thirty, I keep seeing him become more aware and grow. The commercial success is nice, but more important is that he outlines his own path, from within himself and his own responsibility.

This is how he runs his company: everyone is responsible for his or her own life. He does so with an open mind, knowing that one of his team members can become an entrepreneurial leader themselves. They, in turn, can work with their own team to invent, create, sell. The chances he has got himself, that he himself was allowed to take on as an entrepreneur, he also wishes for his team members.

Everyone's path to self-realization is different. As a manager you can only accept what the path of the other is and support him on it, without undermining your own purpose as an entrepreneurial leader. To know which is the best choice to make or how you deal with the choice of someone else, you need self-knowledge and self-awareness.

As a coach you would not stop a football player who can take the step from Anderlecht to Barcelona. As a coach, and an entrepreneurial leader, you can see how you could work with Barcelona, where your own team also gets a boost. I myself have experienced something similar. I was registered at the judo club in Gellik, the village where I lived with my parents and little sister. When I was twelve my coach, Frits Ceulemans, told me: 'To give you and your ambition every chance, I have to let you go. Maybe I can bring you to the level of Belgian champion, but after that there is nothing more to learn here for you. For the next step you need another coach. Go now, guilt-free, you're always welcome here. I remain your biggest fan. ' It moves me until today. In this way he has made the greatest possible contribution as a coach to my sporting career. I am convinced he silently enjoyed my successes with me. Maybe he really has remained my biggest fan, if that was measurable.

At Cronos I sometimes see that entrepreneurial leaders find it particularly difficult to let their team members take responsibility for their own life. They fear losing them, thus putting themselves at a disadvantage in their short-term drive for creativity. Entrepreneurial leaders want to create, and they like to be recognized for that. But in the long term, they win if they facilitate team members to take responsibility for their own life, even though it causes them to leave.

An example. Rudolf was unable to take the next step with our team and threatened to leave. He was advised to look elsewhere in the group. And yes, another place offered him the opportunity to take a step, whereupon he blossomed again. He has now built a team of twenty employees. Both him and us have won.

Where do you want to go? What are your dreams? How do you want to direct your life? Which script do you want to write? You can take responsibility over your own life, but to create added value with a team, you must know whether you want to fly to Hawaii or Alaska. As an entrepreneurial leader you have the responsibility to map out a path. Without it, there is no team, and no chance of leadership.

Yellow belt
You are the architect
of your own life

Write a life story
based on your own dream
Pass it on vulnerably and without shame
Repeat it a million times if you have to
Make others believe in your dream
So that they participate with their own passion

In every leadership trajectory, people confront themselves. Many have the found courage to look beyond shame at oneself, and to ask themselves why they do the things they do. At those times the urge for progress is greater than the fear of vulnerability. The standstill has been broken.

Erik is a passionate project manager. His life revolves around his work and serving the customers well. During a *leadership journey* in Les Ondes he kept very aloof during dinner. I asked him if he was okay. No, as it turned out, after a conversation with another participant he realized through self-reflection and a value exercise that he did not want to supervise IT projects at all. He missed creating, the beauty, and had not been happy in his job for a long time. Perhaps he never was. He made a good living, supported his family, had a nice house and bought a gadget every now and then: did he have the right to be unhappy? Yet he often felt anger on the way to work, grief, even pain. Do not give in, he told himself. What would the outside world say if he changed course? How would he still be able to support his family if he went looking for something else? And what was that 'something else'?

But the anger was there, the pain, the frustration. At the age of 49 had to he suddenly started to think about the foundations of his life, his constitution as it were. 'Why should I change now? It is what it is, and it is okay like this. ' But the look in his eyes gave him away. He wanted to work with beauty. The next morning, he told me he wanted to move on, take control of his life. He did not know yet how to get started, and it did not matter, I told him. Today Erik runs a company that offers art to hotels. He has built a whole team. It is a success, both in terms of numbers and in terms of experience. Erik is doing things he wants to do.

Why do you do what you do? A person's path is closely related to his or her motivation. If you really could choose from within yourself, would you do this? To become aware of this is to make progress on the path of self-realization. Thinking and feeling: what resonates with your 'inner self', the person who you are in essence?

When determining strategies, an appeal is often made to the *why-how-what* from Simon Sinek. Why does a company exist? How do we fill the 'why' in? And what exactly are we going to do? We will look at Apple for a moment as an example of a *why-how-what* exercise.

Why does Apple exist? What is Apple / Steve Jobs' dream?
To challenge the status quo.
How do they want to do that?

Through beauty and ease of use, by letting hardware and software work together better.
What are they doing?
They make smartphones, computers, tablets.

This seems like a very natural *why-how-what*. It feels intuitively correct and honest, especially when Steve Jobs was still CEO and he could share his dreams with others through storytelling. Any successful leader gives direction, but at Apple Jobs did it clearly and charismatically - according to some also slightly dictatorial. He just made decisions based on the *why* and *how* of Apple; everything that deviated from that was a no-go. He handled his own dream very consistently.

Moreover, he mastered the art of turning that dream into a story. He kept saying that convincingly and consistently. Without doubt, a thousand times, even when others rejected and disbelieved him. At one point he was even fired from his own company, and yet he came back. Again, fighting for his dream, inspiring others with his story, so that they kept going, over and over again. He had understood that without others who also believed in it, his dream would never become reality.

Predecessors on the path of self-realization base their choices on a clear *why* and have a clear story. Companies that are run like this, transcend the daily process and can plan for the longer term.

Since Steve Jobs has disappeared, Apple has been overtaken quite often in terms of innovation, not infrequently by Asian brands. The last few years it has mainly brought out improved versions of existing products. In numbers, Apple does it superbly.

Tim Cook, Jobs' successor, is also saddled with a very tough *legacy*. As an entrepreneurial leader, he focuses on creating financial added value. But does he not then lose sight of the *why*? Does Apple not perpetuate the status quo too much instead of challenging it? Is it then sustainable enough? Succession also causes family businesses to break with the original mission. Well-intentioned they put profit first, the financial survival. But if they leave behind the dream and the story, sustainability is also compromised. Only surviving is not a life.

We find another example to indicate the importance of the *why* at the so-called nerdy opposite of the hip Apple. After forty years Microsoft is still at the top. Many competitors are faltering or have disappeared. One reason: Microsoft had a leader who made every decision weighed against the *why*. Namely: making technology accessible, so that the chance of knowledge and self-development increases in every living room. The best way to fight inequality.

Bill Gates is no longer the CEO of Microsoft, but never denied his roots. On the website of the *Bill & Melinda Gates Foundation* you can see that they strive for 'More equality, starting with the weakest in society'. Of course, that is not exactly the same *why* as Microsoft's, but here too it is about opportunities.

Every human life is equal. Everyone deserves to be at the same starting line. Anyone who does not get there by themselves deserves a push in the back. A framework for the underprivileged so that they too can become an architect of their own lives. A steppingstone to the path of self-realization by increasing their self-reliance, self-determination and self-development. If we would come to the start on an equal footing, then the place where your cradle stood will no longer determine the chance of success. Then it is up to us, our dreams, our motivation and our strengths, to take responsibility for our own lives.

Worth the same, and yet different tools. Talents are disproportionately distributed; passion is not the same everywhere. Yet every person is a unique combination of it. It then comes down to devoting your energy to making the right choices. You should not measure yourself against others all the time. You are incomparable. Once you realize that, you can be the architect of your own life. Writing your own script instead of following a script that the environment imposes on you.

Via this Apple-Microsoft bridge - after all, this book is about connecting - we end up with the importance of our personal *why-how-what*. Finding that out is not that simple. Our *why* and *how* are our foundations, it is who we really are, it determines our 'inner self'. By feeling, acknowledging and experiencing our *why* and *how*, we are able to follow our own path to map out and make choices: which turns should we take, what should we leave?

'Why' is very personal, it is rooted in the emotional center of our brain and is difficult to express in words. Say why seven times and you know your *why*. Easier said than done. When you feel what you do feels natural, then you can be proud that it is consistent with 'why' you do it. Being aware of that makes you more certain if you are faced with a (life) choice.

An entrepreneurial leader who is unaware of his *why* and *how*, finds no satisfaction and will continue to doubt. He will therefore not succeed in creating something in the world from within in a sustainable way. He is guided by the choices, thoughts and life paths of others. He is not and will not be perceived as the architect of his own life. In time, his team will also feel that he no longer reasons, creates, sells and delivers from within. They feel cheated and lose all motivation. That frustration jumps to the (not so much) entrepreneurial leader, because recognition by the environment is not forthcoming. A very vicious cycle.

If you, as an entrepreneurial leader, start from your own life architecture, then you have less need for recognition. You do your thing. You are there for your team, the team is there for you, to invent, create and sell together. In service to each other. Of course, there are always frameworks and rules from others or the organization you have to take into account. An entrepreneurial leader is aware of this and creates harmony in it, so that no counterforces can arise that knock you off course. This also applies to value conflicts with stakeholders, including team members, customers and shareholders, which are almost inevitable. You then have four options:

• To keep your job, you follow the shareholders. With all the negative consequences associated. Your chances of success as an entrepreneurial leader are dwindling significantly.

• You try to convince shareholders of your values: they must follow you. That is difficult. Beliefs are often stuck, because they have become so solidified over the years or because they are deeply personal.

• Within the space that you are given, you try to stick to your own line, whereby the conflicts follow each other. You then have to ask yourself the question whether it is livable, whether your path is compatible with the organization at all. Maybe there are other, better ways. Side note: in elite sports you usually have no option other than the official federations, Olympic Committees and other governing bodies.

• You look at 'what' you can do differently and 'where' that could be to live a life according to your own script. Daring to walk away is hard but necessary if the only option is to stay true to yourself.

Ten minutes after my third-place finish in Sydney - and remember, I was barely twenty years old - a journalist asked: "Is this the start of a great sports career?" To which I replied: ' No, I will quit judo. My big dream is to become a doctor.'

As of today, I am not a doctor, but judo at the highest level did not give me a sense of accomplishment or satisfaction anymore. My 'why' was one big question mark. Elite sport had been a way to bring out the best in myself. To turn my potential into a meaningful life. But at some point, only an innate talent remains, without the passion. Too much had happened that was inconsistent with my values, somewhere along the way I had lost my passion. And talent alone does not make you the best of the world. You must be stimulated by encounters, events, environments.

Orange belt
A goal is a dream
with a deadline

(From Napoleon Hill)

A goal energizes your dream,
makes it executable
An entrepreneurial leader
is inspired by his dreams
He withstands the pressure of his environment
And does not try to control the future
He creates the future by visualizing it

When we are aware that we are responsible for our own life, we can start directing our lives. How do we do that? How can we keep pursuing our dreams with focus? For an entrepreneurial leader it is not simple either. Making the translation from the emotional brain (*why* and *how*) to the rational, verbal, can be done through the SMART goals.

Specific
Measurable
Attainable

Relevant
Time-bound

An example. 'I would like to go on an adventure holiday with my partner.' If the *why is*: I always want to learn, and the *how*: I want to do that through *experience*, then this is not a SMART objective. It is not specific enough. Where are you going for the holidays? For how long? What kind of vacation? Why together? It is also not measurable. The only thing that could be measured is whether or not you've been on vacation, and if so, has something of your *why* been fulfilled? The objective is acceptable and realistic: going on vacation with your partner. It is not bound in time. When do you go on holiday? Next week, in a year?

It is critical for an entrepreneurial leader to transition from *why* and *how* to be able to make to *what*, time and again from within (*why-how*) to working outside (*what*). I often come across leaders who are unaware of the responsibility for their own lives and have forgotten how to dream.

On the leadership journey in Les Ondes, we do the 'exercise of the dream catcher'. In one-on-one conversations we dig for their deepest motivation, their life wish. "Tell me about your dreams." There is a lot of resistance to that. People refuse to open up. 'We are not here for that?' They want to become entrepreneurs, build the best sales team. Also, in workshops I ask them to write down dreams and discuss them with someone. Without the slightest limitation, as big or as crazy as they may be. It is an exercise that invites all rational arguments to move aside, think like a child again, have the courage to let them get to know you, to make that connection beyond shame. The value of it should not be underestimated: daring to show your dreams to the world.

For example, someone in Les Ondes came to me, she was about 35 years old and was about to switch from team member to team leader. She had difficulty with the exercise of the dream catcher, she did not understand how you could become a better team leader by dreaming. Is it not your duty as leader to get your team from A to B in the most efficient way? I could agree with her reasoning. A grown woman stood in front of me had been told that for thirty years that you especially are not allowed to dream, and at a later age that you must be functional and preferably work as hard as possible. I reassured her that these journeys serve to leave old habits, reset and watch how to take the next step. I invited her to stop the struggle and surrender to the flow. Dare to dream.

Okay, but why also write them down? To connect with yourself. Pronounced dreams say a lot about who you are, what you want and how you can become the architect of your own life. Many avoid the responsibility to get started with it. There are a thousand and one apologies for that. Dreams are for pre-schoolers. We adults have to work hard. Doing things right, that's what it is all about (efficiency); whether we are doing the right things (effectiveness) is not important. Carry your burden, stop dreaming and you earn your place in heaven.

But you need dreams to come up with opportunities. As entrepreneurial leader you cannot live without them. Otherwise, you cannot act on it with your team and try new things. Surfing along on the wave of efficiency is not something you can do as an entrepreneurial leader. It is essential to keep checking what is already there, what you learned with your team from previous experiments and in which direction to guide them for a relevant next step. You do that from your own action. But then of course you have to know where you want to go. Planning your path starts with catching a dream.

Entrepreneurial leaders want something tangible, visible, to have done something noticeable in their career, they want to leave something behind. Because to approach the ultimate goal, they must have achieved tangible things in the short or medium term. Milestones on their path.

A Goal is a Dream with a Deadline. To clarify this, I go back to my top sporting past. I was five years old and was finally allowed to 'Judo', following the boy next door - he was a year older than me. Combat sports, such a little girl? My parents did not expect so much stubbornness. And so I was on the judo mat for the first time on August 5, 1985, right on my fifth birthday. The following 25 years they would hardly get me off it. Sweating, crying, bleeding. I wanted to win gold at the Olympic Games, just like Ingrid Berghmans. I did not know what all that meant, but however young, the dream was clear.

The dream helped me to keep going, even when the going got tough. I never gave up. In the morning before school started, I went for a walk. No parties or jokes. Friendships had to give way, a normal childhood was not possible. I chose my study in function of judo. My dream determined my life.

But in order to take steps in that direction, you must have concrete goals. Olympic gold was not enough, you have to cut your dream into smaller goals and milestones. Otherwise the path will blur. In the beginning it was the Belgian tournaments and championships in the youth series. Later European matches and competitions. The dream became more concrete. And then

I was selected to try to qualify for Sydney two years later. I was eighteen and just European junior champion. Without realizing it fully, my dream had become a goal with a deadline.

From dream catcher to SMART plan, it is not obvious for everyone. But for an entrepreneurial leader it is a basic pillar. You cannot keep yourself motivated if you do not set a deadline and intermediate objectives. You can graft well-founded choices on this for what you do or do not do. You are forced to think about the near future, about impending decisions and their implications, about any incidents and your reactions to them.

Based on their dream catcher, I let participants write down their goals for one year and divide them into a number of domains; work, relationships, family, health, personal development ... What do you want to put extra energy into in the coming year? Which domains will get less attention? That way they make a goal of their dream and put a deadline on it. A mood board helps to visualize the goals. You collect all kinds of images and texts that reflect the atmosphere and content of display the goal you want to achieve. You make a collage of that, not too neatly arranged. It can be a bit loose, even if you like. Anytime when it gets difficult, the mood board serves as a reminder. It makes a concept, idea or feeling tangible, gives you a better view of the steps you can take to achieve the goal. You can create a mood board for everything: whether you want to run a marathon, dream of another job or want to write a book.

During journeys I still see too many people who want to take the step to entrepreneurial leadership without getting their objective clear. And then the tendency arises to control that future, instead of creating it. That is nevertheless the strength of a successful, entrepreneurial leader: creating the future. The entrepreneur must act from himself, from his own dreams, come up with new things and shape those together with his team.

A non-entrepreneurial leader first looks at the imposed strategy and the budgets, and then draws up a plan. In this way he can partly get a grip on the future, on paper or in an *Excel sheet*. The danger is that leaders who cannot or do not want to create the future, try to control it by adopting an authoritarian attitude. That results in conservative leadership.

An entrepreneurial leader sees the strategy of the shareholders or the board of directors as the framework within which to work, but he starts from his own dream. He wants to successfully create with a team. Of course, he has a duty to stay within a framework, he must be accountable and care for his team. Keep communicating: is he still on the right track? But when a Board of Directors, a monitoring committee or the shareholders' have confidence in a leader to create, in order for the enterprise to become stronger, then it is their duty to give him space. To convert his or her dreams into goals and deadlines. The strategy can always be adjusted, but if a Board of Directors or the shareholders keep the reins too tight, there is no entrepreneurial leadership.

Why is it that leaders are no longer allowed to dream? It is one of the downsides of capitalism, I think. That it is the only system that succeeds in improving the living standards of as many people as possible, is obviously a good thing. But capitalism still places knowledge far above dreams, the cognitive suppresses the creative, reason before emotion. It is about the facts and not what makes people tick. The homo economicus does not dream. He only sees added value in financial terms, such as profit maximization. Thinking should only be functional, as little as possible emotional. But the homo sapiens is also a feeling animal. Every person wants to dream and needs the mental space to do so. Without this, you are trapped in a system of external control, that has the consequence that everyone focuses on their tangible rights (salary, company car, holidays ...) instead of on his moral duties. And that applies both for the leader and his team. The financial and the material cloud what really matters: progress.

GREEN BELT
Grab the wheel
Be aware of your strengths and your weaknesses
Bet fully on your strengths
Only then can you give yourself direction
And turn a dirt road into a paved path
Make sure that the climb does not become a pitfall

What is the definition of passion? I'm not even getting into that. By defining it, you limit it. Because this book is mainly based on personal experience, I try to describe passion on the basis of two examples. I take my friend Wim and myself as test subjects.

In the yellow belt we talked about *why* and *how* as representatives of who we really are, what it is all about for us and how we arrive at what is the essence in life for us. Unchangeable.

The orange belt showed how we can express and exploit ourselves, by converting our dreams into concrete goals, by placing posts on our life path. That's our *what*. Changeable. You could see passion see as the water on which the *why* and *how* float. It is the thrust that makes you go for a goal. Without a passion for judo, I would never have been able to bear all that pain to qualify for the Olympics.

The *why* of Wim contribute to the sustainable progress of his environment. His *how*: having an impact through new knowledge and creativity to invent things, to pioneer, to motivate and inspire others, thinking sustainably ahead, placing the environment above the individual, always from a personal approach. His *what*: inventing, establishing, running innovative initiatives.

Technology and science have been his passion for twenty years. The *why* and *how* are excellently served by it, as he uses technology and science to strive for progress. Technology helps him invent new things, he can motivate others through technology and science to work on new things. This increases his impact and contributes to social progress.

If the Cronos Group is an ecosystem, then Wim also provides the breeding ground for all kinds of initiatives to develop further. Businesses are conceived, germinate and grow. It is currently his *what*, but as mentioned, that can change, as opposed to *why* and *how* that relate to our innate strengths, our talents and qualities.

To succeed in making your dreams come true, spread over a series of intermediate goals, you need to know where your strengths lie. That self-awareness is the base coat. Only then can you become an architect of your own life. As a judoka I had an innate talent, plus I had a passion for the game. As a result, I could give up a lot for it and I could continue to train hard. In addition, I enjoyed the support of my environment.

Because of my experience as an elite athlete, I am convinced that you are only able to make your dreams come true when you focus on the things you do well. Just because of the challenges that come your way, it is mentally and emotionally very tough to keep developing yourself in that one talent. If we're honest, a lot of people do not have that patience. It takes strength, courage, passion, vulnerability and spirit. Aspiring, enterpreneurial leaders may recognize this. Ten thousand hours of deliberate practice is needed to reach the absolute top in a discipline. That is what Swedish psychologist K. Anders Ericsson claimed in 1993. That means twenty hours a week for ten years.

In my opinion, it takes about twice as long to really consolidate that climb. Keep going, even when the going gets tough, when the growth slows, the perspective narrows. Both the enterpreneurial leader and the elite athlete are confronted with it. There is a difference that an entrepreneurial leader can stay at the top much longer and on top of that can continue to build because he or she is hardly limited by physical possibilities. While for the elite athlete that has peaked, the black hole threatens. Unfortunately, that is not a myth.

As an elite athlete, you sacrifice everything for that one dream for twenty years, which makes you slowly lose connection with your other talents. You have mastered something, but that concentration of talent and passion weakens you in other areas. Your mastery in judo does not guarantee anything off the mat. It is not a life insurance policy. Often your body determines when it has been enough, and your sports career ends prematurely.

After you have said goodbye to elite sports, you must make a choice: what am I going to do from now on? Where can I revisit so much passion to develop another talent that has been neglected all these years? Do I even want to excel at something again? Does that make sense? And more importantly: do I feel like starting again from scratch, investing ten thousand hours or more to get another to reach the top?

The fact that you are now much older is an advantage: your cognitive ability has increased. But it is also a disadvantage: your mind is less free, you become more defined by limitations from your environment, also from yourself. You have tasted what it is like to be the best at something as an athlete; that aftertaste must not become bitter. Making a dream come true requires passion and patience, blood, sweat and tears. It is by no means a soft path.

Many do not succeed at even making one dream come true. While elite athletes are expected to do it again after their first heroic effort. They know how to do it anyway and they have it the perseverance for it. They can handle anything. But is that really so? I doubt it. It is not because an elite athlete has the drive to go for gold that he can later excel at something else with the same intensity. You cannot have the same passion for every innate talent. You can only be the best in one world. A lot more world awaits beyond that. After I quit judo, I lacked the energy to take a new path. I did not see, was not aware that you never really see the path. What I did feel: an urge to build, to do something - in the widest possible sense. I had not thought about becoming an entrepreneur yet.

I have had to learn to accept that an end point is also a new beginning. That there is a life after sports, that not everything is a struggle or is about winning. That there may be another path that is also mine. Not that of my partner, colleague or acquaintance, but a personal path of life that I deliberately choose to walk based on the talents I have. Without the medals, without a view of a podium. Not one top, but an infinite mountain range of rising and falling. On the path is the way.

Many former athletes have a hard time making that click and to say goodbye to fame. That is why they are making a comeback. They know they have tons of talent and passion for that one thing and hope to end up on the highest podium again. It is where many an athlete lives for and is willing to go very far, with the risk of mental and physical destruction.

Finding a second dream is not an easy task, continuing in sports as a coach is not either. The waning star needs to be supportive, in the shadow of another. If he or she still cherishes the passion to compete himself, to win, it becomes very difficult. As a coach, a former athlete has to start from someone else's dreams instead of from his own dream. He or she is not used to that. The best judoka in the world will not quickly become the best judo coach in the world. As a midfield athlete you are often better prepared for a role as second violin. And you have less issue with letting others shine.

Just to recap: the green belt comes with your self-awareness strengths. Only then can you learn to use it every day and have the endless patience and laser focus to build something sustainable.

To pave the path of entrepreneurial leadership.

Pitfalls for the entrepreneurial leader

An enterprising leader starts from himself and his own dream and has the enthusiasm to take others with them. Because to be able to, he must have a clear picture of himself and where he wants to go. My Olympic adventure in Sydney shows that your odds for success increase when you complement that self-awareness with an understanding of the other, in where he or she wants to go, what his or her strengths and weaknesses are.

Do not know yourself and the opponent,
and you have hardly any chance of winning
Know yourself but not the adversary
and you have a 50 percent chance of winning
Do not know yourself, but the adversary does,
and you have a 50 percent chance of winning
Know yourself and the opponent,
and you have the greatest possible chance of winning

However, an entrepreneurial leader can also easily fall into a number of traps. Why do I say 'easily' here? The mindset of an entrepreneurial leader is focused on making his dream come true, he wants to win. But by focusing on that, he sometimes loses sight of the bigger picture. His focus is clear: create something together with a team and put it on the market. He is very passionate about this and goes for it one hundred percent. Without that total commitment, he knows he can never win the fight against himself, the other and transcend the environment, and cannot realize his dream. As an athlete I had an Olympic dream that I really wanted to see achieved and for which everything had to give way. Including a normal childhood, or what society considers an average childhood.

Sometimes, however, an entrepreneurial leader is so ambitious that he stumbles over his own ambition. Below I have listed some pitfalls that an entrepreneurial leader has to contend with, and that I have experienced myself in my career and during the coaching of entrepreneurs to be.

Taking on too many tasks

In his ambition to make his dream come true, an entrepreneurial leader often has the idea that he can do it better than his team members or his environment. As a result, he hardly gets around to delegating and uses more energy than necessary. He burns himself up. While his team members have to contend with the crumbs that fall off the table. There is no reciprocal nourishment.

No attention to self-care

Consumed by ambition, an entrepreneurial leader often realizes too late that he wastes his energy. That eats away at his health, both physically and mentally. He ignores warning signs. His drive slows down. The flame fades out slowly.

Squeezing the team

Because an entrepreneurial leader himself is at the center of the action and is so focused, he can lose touch with the other and the environment. He no longer knows how his team members are doing and progressively makes them into pawns that fuel his own ambition, forgetting that they too dream of the next step on their path to self-realization. The entrepreneurial leader is off, the team tries to follow but has to drop out. He wears his people out. Not much later, he himself runs out of steam or electricity. Even if he still wins, he is lost.

Thinking of nothing new

Racing against the clock, he forgets the Kairos time. He only resides in the rational, hard, functional and no longer connects with the emotional, soft, creative. As a result, he no longer succeeds in coming up with new things and is forced to fall back on the old box of tricks. Rinse and repeat, that is not future-oriented business.

Not listening empathetically

Empathetic listening is very effective, but it takes time. It is an investment in people that pays off in the longer term. Sometimes an entrepreneurial leader forgets the value of empathetic listening. Over time he might still be leading but is no longer a leader. You do not convince people of your story if they feel that you, as a leader, are not really interested in them. This way, they will not get a chance to make the dream come true.

A matter of shared recognition

The entrepreneurial leader craves recognition, but his team members also get demotivated if they are not seen or heard. Recognition can include tangible things like pay raise, a great party, a team building weekend. But just as important, if not more important, are the shared moments when there is mutual attention. If as an entrepreneurial leader you do not listen to your team or your environment, you do not open yourself up to get to know the other better and how he or she looks at the world, it will become difficult to create support in the long term. Why would anyone make an effort for you if you make no effort for him or her? The great strength of an entrepreneurial leader is that he gathers people around him who are happy to work for him, follow his vision with their heart. You can never lose that credit. First the human capital, then the money.

No long-term vision

One of the core jobs of an entrepreneurial leader is to find the right moment to tell his story from his dream. He offers a direction that people want and can follow. A framework within which it is pleasant for everyone to work. That can include a treaty of rights and responsibilities. It creates clarity. You know where you stand. However, an enterprising leader can stack his plate so full that he no longer sees what is happening around him, let alone where it needs to go. You do not develop vision with short-sightedness.

Welcome to Les Ondes
On a journey to yourself

This is the heart of the book, literally and figuratively. The passage is in the middle in the book and it is about a place where lifelines converge and leave. People find themselves and their dreams, doubters become entrepreneurs, followers grow into leaders. Nothing is necessary, everything is allowed. Here you can feel the true heartbeat of the Cronos Group. You learn to dance to your own rhythm, instead of obeying an imposed pace.

Several times a year I travel with a group of passionate young women and men - fresh blood - to the Ardennes. We call it a leadership journey. One is in sales, the other dreams of entrepreneurship, a third wants to take the plunge from team member to team leader. Whatever their background, they have one thing in common: they are ready for the next step in their lives. The journey takes them to Les Ondes, our home in Nadrin, a village near La Roche of less than a thousand souls. Two hotels, one of which has become a haunted house, a ribbon of houses winding around the church, the baker gradually extinguishing his oven, a pharmacist, and a dwindling soccer club. The youth leaves, the peace remains.

The authentic *Résidence* is basic but comfortable. Lots of wood, heavy chairs - you can barely move them. As for the tables, do not even try. Time has also stood still there. When you enter, you immediately smell that typical chalet scent, a combination of forest air and fireplace. You reach the rooms via a narrow staircase, which of course creaks under your feet. It keeps catapulting me back to the youth hostels where I went to sports camp as a teenager. The higher you go, the more it looks like Villa Cockatoo. The memory of Pippi Longstocking always pops up in Les Ondes. "I've never done it, so I think I can." Her motto would not be out of place on the wall of that house that offers peace, warmth and radiates safety. A place that makes you believe that anything is possible, as long as you believe in it yourself.

It is so chill that your heart rate drops ten beats by itself. Sink in the blue fabric seats. Books and magazines that visitors have left behind are everywhere. Surrounded by grass, shrubs and trees, as if you were right in the middle of a green lung. The bar is straight out of a brown village cafe – you get sucked into it, although it is far from an acceptable hour for a glass. You can almost taste the connection. Sit and enjoy, it is what is on offer.

Elsewhere on the domain are some log cabins. In the backyard it is wonderful to relax in the Finnish sauna and hot tub. A big, covered terrace has thirty of those massive chairs and tables. Unyielding. They are arranged around two enormous fireplaces. During winter barbecues the only source of heat, a soft glow when the summer evening threatens to get a bit chilly. Nothing tastes better here than the local beer.

Fairytale-like and yet very tangible. Built in Ardennes stone, decorated in a green carpet of ivy, surrounded by hundred-year-old trees. A robustness that offers support in turbulent times. The house on the banks of the river Ourthe forces you to slow down. By taking distance, you suddenly see things sharper. Accelerate by slowing down. The time is given plenty of space, and vice versa. Chronos and Kairos are leapfrogging. In Nadrin there is no station. Long before you arrive, you have to leave behind the daily express train.

Close to Les Ondes is a rock wall, Le Hérou. With its ninety meters it dominates the wildly meandering Ourthe between La Roche-en-Ardenne and Houffalize. A beautiful, mysterious site, classified as Walloon heritage, with an exceptional, imposing panorama. You reach this artwork of nature after a long, treacherous hike with steep slopes. Over the years Le Hérou has become sort of my hero, steady as a rock. Here travel companions become soul mates.

Everyone is invited to descend the mountain wall. Backwards. Of course, professionally secured. Fear of heights or not, for everyone it is a threshold they have to cross. The Ourthe churns beneath you while you hang almost horizontally in a harness. In the flow of the descent, you can even enjoy it. The exercise symbolizes the courage to step over that edge all the way through vulnerability and dependence and take the plunge into the unknown. You will come across these thresholds on your path to self-realization, which in hindsight you made bigger than they really were, that challenge you and make you grow. And you learn that trust in others is both a springboard and a safety net.

A little further, right in the middle of a flat terrain, 'the pamper pole' rises up, ten meters high, a foot thick, with narrow steps around it. The participants can climb it, one step at a time, in safe conditions. When I describe it like this it seems like child's play, but I can assure you that your courage drops several times on the way. Once at the top, ten meters high, you have to stand on the pole. From a squat to an upright position. On the ground, a toddler could do it with ease, but once up there many get fearful.

"Just do it now!" It is easy to shout from below. It shows little empathy. Which seems very simple to one person, can be extremely difficult for the other. It is an insight that also a supervisor consciously carries with him every day. Not just team members, also team leaders should be put in front of and on that pole. So they understand that it is not always the people who have a disability, but that the environment limits them, so that they no longer cross a threshold. If we would also look at people who do have a mental or physical limitation, we might take their challenges into consideration, and adapt the environment to them.

As soon as you get up on top of the pole, you face the following challenge: jump to a trapeze two meters further into the thin air. I have not yet succeeded in this. Partly due to my small body, but also a deeper fear: I am just not capable of this. Every time when I stand up on that pole, my eyes fill. Time and again I risk it, I touch the trapeze, but cannot grab it. And then I find myself dangling in my safety harness.

While I was once celebrated on an Olympic podium, the pamper pole stays completely stoic. He is equally inflexible to everyone. This is not about fighting someone, about winning, about being the best at it something, but about trying, creating, undertaking, dancing, life. Overcoming yourself.

The underlying meaning is as a pole above water – below in the valley, the Ourthe continues to flow undisturbed: if you want to succeed, you have to believe in yourself, get past doom scenarios
that you talk yourself into. Every time I float there, supposedly failed, I think: it wasn't that bad, with a little more confidence you could have done it. And now you're swinging from a trapeze, ten meters above the ground. Much more fun anyway. We are our own biggest opponents. A lot of potential remains untouched because we have not started an assignment confidently enough.

After the pamper pole we return to the tranquility of Les Ondes. Some very proud, others disappointed, but there is a large mug of hot chocolate waiting for everyone. It can be so simple. Just like the first sip of water after the weigh-in for an important judo competition could make me intensely happy. That is all I needed. Even if only for a moment, because then the bell rang: I had to win another fight. In Les Ondes nothing was needed after the chocolate milk. The row of 'cold and sweaty shoes' the entrance have something in common. We all face challenges in life, challenges that are not quite equal, but must be considered as equal. Those who handle it best, will learn to use their potential optimally on the way to self-realization.

Les Ondes means 'the waves' in French. Ebb and flow, of rapids to delayed time, restlessness becomes rest. Here you can be yourself, as a follower and as a leader, as a complete person.

In her book *Kairos, the new inspiration* philosopher Joke Hermsen describes the distinction that the ancient Greeks made between Kairos, the inner, subjective experience of time that can heal, and Chronos, the objective, measurable time that determines when something is allowed or not. We mainly live according to the Chronos time. If you are not fast enough, you will lose. You become continuously hunted, a rat race against time. According to Hermsen we have become victims of it, I would even call it slaves. Our well-being suffers from the overriding pressures of non-stop efficiency. In this way, valuable insight and effort are lost.

Admitting Kairos requires a different mindset. It is a form of art of living, being in the now with your thoughts and your soul, in full consciousness. The environment no longer constitutes a limitation, even seems to disappear. The flow and concentration that flow from this lead to new, creative insights. We experience such moments when we are daydreaming, staring ahead of us, taking a walk or bike ride through nature, immersing yourself in music, meditating, contemplating, reflecting. In Kairos time I learned to enjoy judo. Martial arts became an art of living that far transcended the tatami. With respect for yourself and the environment.

Fighting in Chronos time is all about the result – with all the suffering and pain that comes with it. Under Chronos everything becomes 'by necessity', as life against time often feels, timed. All the time I was in Japan without letting myself go in their rhythm, in their view of judo, in the sport as a dance... I want to be a champion even in training. It was a constant battle against an imaginary threat. Those four weeks in Japan were always a punishment, without any privacy or contact with home - there were no mobile phones or e-mail yet, I had to make do with one fax per week. In Kairos time my experience would have been completely different. I would have lived more.

Joke Hermsen calls for a break away from Chronos. To slow down. Without guilt or shame to give yourself that chance. It is not the intention that we completely withdraw ourselves from the world. That has no use. The question is rather how we learn to switch between slow and fast. Losing track of time to be able to see clearly again. A pitstop is done to continue racing afterwards. Catch your breath and start dancing. The balance between equivalent time experiences, is where the key to self-realization, well-being, sustainable well-being and ultimately social progress lies.

In Les Ondes, the participants put away their smartphones and other devices, even their watches. Here Kairos gets all the time. I notice it on every trip which I organize: as soon as the participants lets go of their resistance, they really connect with themselves, become calm and creative. It is often the people who let themselves be driven by Chronos who think they do not need a disconnect. They imagine themselves in a comfort zone. But only when they dare to leave it, do they discover true comfort. To truly connect with yourself, you have to break free from your surroundings. Leave your world behind for a moment. What at first seems like a waste of time becomes time savings. During such a journey, more happens than you think. The relaxation lays the foundation for the effort.

Not easy, because our living environment is often the perfect excuse not to be concerned with ourselves. The technology 'helps' with this: no time for boredom anymore, everything as efficiently as possible. And yet we have never had so little time. In Les Ondes, on the other hand, we follow the wave motion, we learn to balance between result and process, between the linear, measured time and the inspired, inner time, between action and reflection, between rapids and deceleration. Here you go on a journey to yourself. To really come home.

Apart from yourself
supportive leadership in three belts

The base
Support the other, separate from yourself
Amor Mundi
Learn to listen
Self-determination

Thanks to its adaptability, capitalism has managed to survive crisis after crisis. But has the limit not been reached? Can companies keep their head above water in this constant flow of information? Is self-development still possible without social awareness? Aren't we all a collective project? The limited resources for survival are running out slowly and the constant war for talent mainly makes victims.

Even on Wall Street there is a growing realization that companies do not just add value for shareholders to pursue, but also interests serving employees, customers and the wider community. Profit cannot be the only goal. Greed gives way to sustainability, diversity and well-being. A company is not an island but a part of society. In addition to entrepreneurial leadership, there is a need for a different kind of leadership. A model that supports well-being, growth and entrepreneurship of the other. Supportive leadership, that triggers, inspires, motivates, stimulates, facilitates, activates. Supportive leaders consciously choose to help, even serve, the other, in the interest of their well-being. That is contagious. From person to person, to all of humanity. Someone who is in his or her immediate environment lucky enough to be able to work with a supportive leader will learn to live and work healthier, wiser and more autonomously.

To the extent possible, parents at first should be supportive leaders. A child wants to grow from a dependent baby to an independent, confident adult who stands on strong foundations in life. A parent who assumes the role of supportive leader, will be able to guide him / her much better in this than a 'curling parent', who time and again sweeps the irregularities, the bumps and the pits, off the path of the growing child. But you cannot learn to jump without hurdles.

To be able to take steps in life towards self-reliance it is of paramount importance that growing children learn to cope with obstacles. Success or failure, they must at least make the effort. Only then do they get stronger and bigger. Curling parents do just the opposite. They smooth out all paths. Their spoiled children get the idea that the world is sterile and clean, that only success stories are written, that life will run smoothly. A curling parent's goal: make it as easy as possible for his or her growing child, rather than create a framework within which the child can experiment, explore, make mistakes, learn from it and improve themselves.

Amor Mundi

A counterpart to Amor Sui (egocentric), Amor Mundi (altruistic) explains the basis for supportive leadership. In the words of Hannah Arendt, the great twentieth-century philosopher and political thinker who pierced totalitarian systems:

Without love and responsibility for the world (Amor Mundi) insufficient counterbalance can be offered to the Amor Sui, the selfishness, which is considered the primacy of capitalism. We only become free and 'human' if we dare to put our private interests aside. We should not only dare to ask ourselves: 'What can you do for me? ', but above all dare to ask ourselves:' What can I do for you? '

Conscience is that part of you that judges good and evil. You could call it your 'inner self', the self-conscious core, the voice within that guards the connection with yourself. This whispering voice
is in stark contrast to the garish ego that tends to be tyrannical and dictatorial behavior. The advantage of starting from conscience is that it is independent of your origin, race, religion, gender and even from the time in which you live. As a result, working from your conscience is

automatically sustainable. It also allows you to let go.

That is the opposite of working from your 'ego', which is very time and situation bound and is intrinsically discriminatory and not sustainable. The ego focuses on its own survival and satisfaction, often by controlling the environment. People who start from their ego do not mind excluding others, as long as they can manage to fulfil their own ambition. The ego protects us from the outside world that it divides into threats and opportunities. In other words: the ego is not always negative, for it also protects us from danger. It ensures that we are not 'used' or 'abused' by others. That we do not let ourselves be pushed around or that we are not too nice to someone with bad intentions.

But the ego does have a larger, negative connotation. It does derail people, so that they only think about themselves and forget that others also know and can do something. That way they push others to the side for their own benefit. Egocentric people put themselves in the center of attention, they are the center of their world, no longer aware that other people live around them. They have become their ego.

All too often, however, it is a forced facade behind which uncertainty hides about who they really are. Because they never really thought about where they actually want to go, because they never dared to take responsibility over their own lives. They do not know who there is under the shell of their ego, pretending not to care to know either. As if, because deep down lurks the fear that they have been cheating themselves all their lives. They perform according to what social norms expect of them, always looking for recognition from the outside - which they do not always get. That unfulfilled desire, the lack of recognition, causes enormous frustration. Frustrations which in turn are the trigger of even more negativity, such as addictions, anger and violence.

People who live according to their ego lose themselves and do not know what to do with their sorrow. Yet they especially have a need for that but never learned to express it. Their ego, the shield on which they have hoisted themselves, turns against them. Their survival is their downfall. They are homesick for themselves, but they do not know anymore where home is. What remains is a false sense of security and control, at least in their profiling to the outside world. Because instead of leading, they stand alone. Isolated. Alienated, also from themselves.

As a counterbalance to the ego, you rely on conscience every time you put the development of the other first. Conscience shows you the environment in terms of a community. Self-interest is not the most important, but the contribution you can make to the sustainable well-being of the collective. Whether that is a team, a company, an organization or the whole of society. Where ego constantly puts itself first, conscience is the social counterpart that takes into account the environment. Anyone who manages to put their ego away from time to time will feel physically and mentally lighter, become enlightened. You can think clearly about the sustainable well-being of each fellow human being. A supportive leader sails on his conscience; he will ask what he can do for someone, instead of weighing up what the other can bring him. No matter how worthy the goal you pursue, if it is to the detriment of others, a supportive leader will not do it.

Relying on his conscience, a supportive leader will also share. He shares his knowledge and skills, his wisdom and often also his economic wealth. He does this because his conscience made him aware has of the fact that we are all connected and, in some way, dependent on each other. As a result, we start to care for each other. With compassion and compassion. So that the other does not cross his cross only need to wear. Shared sorrow is less sorrow.

Believe it or not, it is also the message with which Jesus showed himself as a supportive leader. Or more specifically: Nelson Mandela who sacrificed himself for the greater good, disappeared for years behind bars and yet did not become bitter. He never wanted to get revenge. Even when he became president, he gave everyone equal opportunities, white or black, even his opponents. Compare that with potentates like Trump or Putin, who are merely pursuing short-term success based on their own ego. And yet always remain unsatisfied.

Learn to listen

Even the supportive leader has an ego - without it he would not survive. But when appropriate, he can put it aside. He is not blindly driven by his own ambition, by which he is able to listen empathetically and mindfully.

An empathetic listener listens to learn. He is genuinely interested in the other and does not listen from his own self or ambition. He listens to learn things about the other, who he or she really is, how he or she thinks from his or her background and personality. The goal: to help others and give them confidence. Very often people listen just to be able to answer again. They are constantly, in their own thoughts, checking off what they will say, based on who they are, what story they can tell and how to get attention back to themselves again.

Mindful listening goes one step further. It is simply listening. Without wanting to help, but completely at the service of the other, being completely there for the other. By listening, you can leave it to the other feel that he or she is important, that they matter and that they are completely fine just the way they are. In the next part I will go into this in more detail.

Self-determination, after Deci and Ryan

Supportive leadership facilitates other people's self-realization. A supporting leader is intrinsically motivated in this; he does something because he likes it, not because he's motivated from the outside to do. I like to refer to the Self Determination Theory of Edward L. Deci and Richard Ryan. That theory examines the underlying reasons behind the choices people make from within themselves, without being influenced by external factors. The individual behavior with which people motivate themselves and from where they act. Self-realization.

External factors that stimulate and activate humans are called extrinsic motivators. Within organizations, these can be in the form of accepting bonuses, annual figures, evaluations and references. Also, the opinion that colleagues have of you belongs to this category. People are also motivated and stimulated from within. Personal interest, curiosity, the urge to learn something are intrinsic motivators. They form the breeding ground for passion, creativity and persistence.

The degree of self-determination is based on the mutual relationship between extrinsic and intrinsic motives. The Self-Determination Theory states that man is an active organism that wants to improve itself and get to a higher level. That development is a natural process, though it does not happen automatically. The process requires continuous input and support. The social context or the circumstances can either grow or hinder this psychological growth. The tension between man and his social context determine his behavior, experiences and developments.

According to self-determination theory, these are the most desirable and high-quality forms of motivation and involvement: perseverance, improved performance and creativity. To support it, autonomy, competence and connectedness are essential. When one or more of these three are not fed, that will have an adverse effect on well-being.

Autonomy. Or the degree of freedom of choice. The feeling that you have your own life in your hands. It requires constant vigilance from an entrepreneur leader: is there sufficient autonomy? At Wingmen, for example, where I coach young entrepreneurs, we offer mental and financial security so that someone can be entrepreneurial at all times. Their autonomy is not hindered by the fear of failure. The safety net is there. In my opinion, autonomy has a lot to do with self-determination. Only in autonomy can you determine what you want to do. It allows you to move forward according to your own values, on your own path.

Connectedness. It is important that people you manage feel a connection with you and with the rest of the team. You want to inform them about what is going on, reward them correctly and give them meaningful work. Your team members and colleagues should feel useful. If that is not the case, their trust in the leader crumbles, even if he is the serving type.

Competence. This refers to the interaction with the environment, the space that you enforce and receive to further develop and demonstrate your abilities. When people feel competent, their well-being and performance improve.

The three BELTs

The evolution from elite athlete to entrepreneur was not an obvious one for me. But at least as an entrepreneurial leader you are still visible, still have some of that applause left. As a supportive leader you also pass that on, and you resolutely step aside to allow someone else a step forward. I struggled with that in the beginning, to trade the limelight for the shade. Luckily, I had the best guides, people who have gone before me on the path, and to whom I am very grateful.

Eddy as an inspiration

As I wrote in the account of that Olympic day in Sydney, Eddy De Smedt was an indispensable, unshakable pillar in achieving my medal. In the preparation for and during the Games itself, he supported me with heart and soul, separate from himself. To make me shine, to make me to leave a mark on the world as an athlete, he continued to believe in me. In defining the three belts of supportive leadership he was a great inspiration.

Supported by Jef

I have been working at the Cronos Group since 2013. In all these years I have had the good fortune to regularly exchange thoughts with Jef De Wit. He helps me in my development as an entrepreneurial leader with building leadership journeys in Les Ondes, he now supports me as a I further develop Wingmen as a supporting leader, as part of the Cronos Group. Leading up to this book, I reflected a lot about his elusive leadership. Once again, he has made me rise above myself to take the next step. It was he who planted the seed from which the path to purpose has grown.

Jef provides tailored guidance based on the person he wishes to support (supportive leadership), but always connected to his own dream (entrepreneurial leadership). He allows the two to merge into an ecosystem that transcends his ego and will outlive him.

Wingmen

In my own incubator I try to be the best possible supportive leader. Wingmen is a safe haven for passionate, future entrepreneurs to find their way and further map it out. We want to provide maximum support to the unique combination of passion and talent that every person is, so that he or she can reach maturity. For this, they can call on a platform of services so nothing distracts them from their passion, from what they are good at and where they can make a difference.

Thanks to the financial support, the entrepreneur does not have to worry about his livelihood. After all, that fear can be so crippling that some no longer even consider venturing into business. The ultimate goal remains self-reliance.

By building Wingmen I learn a lot about myself and others. It is a path that gives a lot of enrichment. Not always easy, not always soft. Often invisible, and for me not in the concrete and
tangible action.

It takes a completely different consciousness than working towards the Olympics Games. With Wingmen I hope to support others in making their own Olympic dream - in the figurative sense of the word - come true. And all that away from myself. It takes more patience than I ever could have expected.

Blue belt
No expectations

If you want to support others selflessly
Then stop the fight against their values
Get out of the world of others
Feel what they need
without even naming it
All at the service of their path to progress

No expectations. An unusual proposition in these times in which we measure an identity based on results achieved. If you wish to empower others as a supportive leader, however, it is impossible to stick to set expectations. The moment we set expectations we decide for the others what we think they should do. The core of supportive leadership lies in empowering the other, the way he or she works, and according to their view of the world. That does not work if we keep imposing our own expectations.

During a judo training in Hooglede in preparation for Sydney I sat crying on a bench at one point. I did not like it anymore: take exams at the university after I traveled all over Europe for ten qualifying tournaments? I was completely exhausted, mentally and physically. Eddy De Smedt from the Olympic Committee came to me and promised to assist. He wanted to support me to make my Olympic dream come true, not as a technical judo coach, but as a mental facilitator.

I recently ran into him when I was in Ostend to support the Belgian Cats - our national basketball women qualified with flying colors for the Olympic Games in Tokyo. I told him about my book and that he was one of my great sources of inspiration. His response: "Our joint journey started long before Sydney, in Hooglede. We took it together and even if you hadn't won that bronze medal, I wouldn't have regretted my choice to help you feel better about yourself." The foundation of supportive leadership.

Eddy has done everything to understand my world, spared no effort to analyze how I functioned and how I reacted to what was happening around me. That enabled him to say the right things when I was blocked, for example after losing my quarter finals.

Have you worked so hard for this?

Are you letting the chance for Olympic glory pass?

Is that what you have to show the world?

Wake up!

And did I ever wake up. He would never have succeeded if he had not spent so much energy on me in those months prior to that day. He had made the choice to support me in making my Olympic dream happen. And he did, starting from my dreams and my strengths. He used his own strengths for it, without before pursuing public recognition. Eddy always tried to find a solution
no matter how intense the emotions got. That is how he acquired huge authority among us as athletes.

Characteristic for a supportive leader like Eddy is helping the other separate from himself, in contrast to the entrepreneurial leader who starts from himself, puts a team at the service of his own dream, his story, and aspires to recognition and success for this.

You can misunderstand the term 'supportive leader'. A supportive leader does not necessarily manage an entire team. It is possible, but it is not necessary. The bottom line is that he can put his own ego aside and play a supporting role in making the dreams come true of people he empowers. Often his influence does not become apparent until after the moment it goes away. Afterwards people realize that he kept things together. Composed characters with an innate gentleness and a lot of empathy find it easier to be a supportive leader. They are goal-oriented and think long term, they know very well what they want without worrying, they have persistence, discipline and patience. Often entrepreneurial leaders do not recognize the place and added value of supporting leaders.

To be free from expectations, it is important that you can place yourself in the world of the other. Very often it is the case that leaders go against the values of their team members, that they try to convince them of their own right and have a conflict for it. Entrepreneurial leaders, above all, want to make their own dream come true. They have a path for that in mind, also for their team. While members of that team have their own dream, want to create from oneself (with or without another team). In their ambition to put something into the world, to show themselves, their own in pursuit of profit, entrepreneurs sometimes lose their dreams and values and the strengths of their team. An entrepreneurial leader often has expectations that are so high that it remains to be seen whether his team will still keep the motivation and resilience to redeem them. That resilience and motivation in turn depend on how much the team can relate to the story of the entrepreneurial leader.

To be able to progress and at the same time guarantee the sustainable well-being of people and society, we need both entrepreneurial and supportive leaders, but also followers. Entrepreneurial leaders encourage creation, so that things are put into action for action and visible results. Supportive leaders watch over the happiness and health of the other. Together they ensure sustainable progress.

Over the years I have experienced both entrepreneurial leadership and supportive leadership. Leadership is a spectrum. Certain young entrepreneurs I have coached run their business like a banana plantation: very focused on efficiency, results and growth. The processes of these companies are optimized, they know exactly what they want to create, how to deliver it and through which sales channels. The entrepreneurial leaders at the head of such companies have a very strong focus, are dealing with the hard results and trying to control every issue. They are visible, active and have clear expectations their team in the short and medium term.

Other entrepreneurs run their business according to the jungle principle, the other end of the business spectrum. These initiatives want to experiment and innovate, their focus is not so much on much making a profit, but on renewing and surviving.

What the banana plantation has in common with the jungle is both models expect things from their team. Without setting expectations, 'banana companies' cannot efficiently provide products and services to the market, sell and deliver. Without expectations, 'jungle companies' cannot invent new services or products and everything related to it. If we look at the path of the entrepreneurial leader, then expectations formed for yourself and for the people around you are an essential pillar. Without expectations you cannot take responsibility for your own dream and nobody will buy into your story.

I found out during the many conversations leading up to this book that some leaders have no expectations of others. They provide freedom and autonomy, do not impose unnecessary pressure. One of those telling moments took place in Les Ondes, where I — as mentioned before – frequently go with young entrepreneurs. Until then the oasis in the Ardennes symbolized a process of awareness for me, in which the participants come to realize that they must claim responsibility for their own lives. That they have goals and expectations aligned to their own strengths, and thus become the architect of their career. It is precisely there, the place where I give workshops about dreams to make it concrete, I came to the insight that as a leader you must not always have expectations. It was so strong that it became the blue belt of the path to purpose as an art of living. This belt is perhaps the hardest to fully grasp, let alone apply, but it can bring the most benefit to the supportive leader, both for itself as for its environment.

It seems like a contradiction, but a supportive leader can move more people forward better if he lets go the expectations in himself and in the other. And that is only possible if he is willing to put himself in the shoes of the other, to let him or her find their own path instead of imposing one. So without him wanting to convince the other that he is right. A supportive leader without expectations has the competence to embrace the world of the other, without standing in the middle of it. He can put his own creative drive on hold and let the other create. He stays in the shadows to let the other to shine. He listens empathetically.

For this, a supportive leader must be capable of thinking long-term (sustainable), without longing for immediate results or instant satisfaction. He must be willing to step out of the action and resist the need to be visible. He leaves the stage to someone else. He looks to the well-being of the people around him and knows that expectations, both towards oneself and towards others, endanger resilience in the long term.

No, Eddy De Smedt had no explicit expectations, but still was he was very proud when I took bronze. Just like many others: national coach Sacha Jatskevitch, his predecessor Jean-Marie Dedecker, the royal couple Filip and Mathilde, my trainer Jean-Jacques, my father in the hall and my mother and sister at home.

Brown belt
Create the framework
As a supportive leader you set the outline
Sometimes you watch, sometimes you pamper
You only intervene structurally when it becomes
precarious
You ease the pain and increase the joy
And above all, you stand by

Create a framework for others, provide resources so that they are closer to make their dreams come true, requires empathy and a lot of flexibility. A supportive leader compliments more than he criticizes. Sometimes you let the other bump against the wall and help take care of the wounds afterwards. A supportive leader picks you up when you're down. He helps you up and repairs wounds, straightens backs and lifts - literally supporting.

In case of success, a supporting leader may or will not want to go on stage. No applause or flowers, his name may be small in the credits to show up. As Howard Behar, the former CEO of Starbucks Coffee Company says: "Let whoever sweeps the floor choose his own broom." As a supportive leader, you make sure there are enough brooms to choose from.

Why is a supportive leader at peace with that: eliminate himself for the benefit of another? Where does he find satisfaction when he is only focused on other people's needs? In the run-up to this book, I wondered about it for a long time and talked to many people about it. Why do some find it important to help others succeed, without getting any kind of recognition - or even respect - for it?

It started to dawn on me more and more that you can also have a lot of impact through others. In some cases more than if you did it just for yourself. Supportive leaders are not looking for direct,
visible recognition in the short term, such as entrepreneurial leaders. Supportive leaders often want to be out of the spotlight, but with a scalable strategy to improve the world. They start from the basic idea that we as humanity have a duty to take care of it so generations after

us will also have a nice life. In general, supportive leaders are not driven by money, power, or direct impact. They focus on the more distant future, think about what the next steps are to contribute to a better world.

What do supportive leaders do differently from entrepreneurial leaders? A supportive leader is committed to the sustainable well-being of the environment or to increase the ecosystem and does so by increasing the well-being of individuals. After all, humanity is the sum of people, where the whole is ultimately more than the sum of its parts.

Regardless of their own short-term dreams, supportive leaders put themselves at the service of others. They help people separate from themselves. They watch over the well-being of their environment. That requires a lot of patience. And an unshakable confidence that they will impact the future by going on that long, gentle path. I think every supportive leader secretly hopes to change the world a bit. Does that not go against the blue belt, 'do not have any expectations'? Not at all, no. You can safely put your hopes on something, and then let go of all concrete, direct expectations.

Perhaps that was also the underlying motive of Eddy De Smedt, the former chief of the Belgian Olympic Interfederal Committee (BOIC) and my counselor in the preparation for Sydney and on site. Perhaps he thought he could change the world of elite sports coaching in Belgium by acting as a supportive leader. He worked on it for thirty years, creating new frameworks within which Belgian athletes could take steps on their path to self-determination, self-reliance and self-development. You can say he succeeded in this several times and with flying colors. The fame was for others, the long-term satisfaction still lingers. Anyone can reap the benefits of his work.

Based on this, you could conclude that supportive leaders make ecosystems grow and evolve in a positive sense. An ecosystem can then be defined as a collection of diverse groups of people who all want to move forward, where

it is safe to experiment and to explore, a fluid structure of springboards and safety nets. In the sports world, for example, these are the different federations
all wanting to 'win' in one way or another. The BOIC is then its umbrella and supporting ecosystem.

Wingmen, the incubator that I was able to set up myself a few years ago under the wing of Jef De Wit, is also an ecosystem of a number of companies. In turn, Wingmen is part of one wider ecosystem, the Cronos Group. Ideally, all those ecosystems intertwine, big and small, and are part of the social fabric of society. Planet Earth is, of course, our primordial ecosystem. Ecosystems come in all shapes and sizes. They can, regardless of their scale, affect a family, a company, a federation or an entire culture. Within every ecosystem entrepreneurial and supportive leaders are required. On the one hand, people who have their own dreams with a team want to deliver in order to achieve progress. On the other hand, supportive leaders who serve their own expectations letting go and creating frameworks for others.

In summary, this brown belt is about creating frameworks to help people make their dreams come true. In time, a supportive leader hopes to contribute to the sustainable well-being of his environment or the ecosystem around it. He strives to have an impact on the future, without the need to make a personal mark or to hand over his business card. Creating positive change, (anonymously or not) contribute to the betterment of the world – or at least part of it - therein lies the true reward for a supportive leader. That's why he makes his own short-term dreams secondary to the dreams of others.

Black belt
Plant the seed
Believe in people and think ahead
Help others believe in themselves
as a supportive leader
Without gnawing at their responsibility
See the future before others create it
Control is good, (allowing to) create better

Plant a seed of confidence in the other person's mind. That summarizes the black belt of the path to purpose in one sentence. But rest assured I have a little more to say about it.

A supportive leader has the power to make the other believe in himself on his path to self-realization. As opposed to entrepreneurial leaders, he is not so much concerned with devising opportunities, but following them to create, sell and deliver. Supporting leaders fully believe in a realizable future. Control is good, (allowing to) create is better. Supportive leaders often see the future before others see it.

Nevertheless, a supportive leader should under no circumstances impose his vision of the future.

After all, thinking ahead sustainably without expectations is his superpower. He tries to give others the confidence that they can do something and come up with opportunities based on who they are themselves and go for it. Do not look back! If it does not work right away, he will be there for to motivate them again. A supportive leader assumes someone's strengths, but he also knows that people need to get the right support to make progress and create from within. Compliments, words of comfort, pep talk, it is all part of it. Which in no way means that he never points out mistakes to his student.

It happens that someone who wants to grow gets stuck, by circumstances, events, experiences or comments from the surroundings. He is, as it were, driven against the bank of the river. A supportive leader makes him realize that he can cope with those external circumstances, so that he gets off the shore and dares to float again in the flow of progress. To help tailor, to inspire to do business without too much pressure and expectations, a supportive leader places people at the center of the organization. Because everyone is different, a standard approach makes no sense. A supportive leader adapts his approach to the needs of the person. Their well-being is the most important. And that starts with making him or her believe in themselves. The mutual confidence becomes the fertile soil in which the seed of collaboration is planted. With the roots in solid soil, you can reach the most light.

Motivating and inspiring others. Massage away the fears and inject faith. A supportive leader eliminates himself for the benefit of the development of others. He empathizes so that they can enjoy themselves. The support he provides is unique, contextual and personal. He constantly takes into account the character and the mental and physical possibilities of the people he helps. In this way he facilitates their growth towards self-determination, self-reliance and self-development - all together: self-realization. This in turn leads to an increase in individual well-being, with the ultimate goal of sustainable well-being for everyone.

People who want to make their dreams come true have the power to create a future that is different, better. Supportive leaders are the invisible pillars who believe unconditionally in people with achievable dreams and the appropriate strengths. They consciously put themselves outside the circle of creation. They applaud when things go well - in silence, because they do not come on stage. They enjoy when others take the next step. They are more concerned with the other than with themselves.

Without patience and self-control, you will not make it as a supportive leader. You have to learn to live without recognition - especially in the short term. You should train and control your ego. Continue to believe in the knowledge and the skills of another, even if he has lost his self-confidence. Not everyone can think and act so altruistically.

Eddy De Smedt is again a textbook example for the black belt of the supportive leader. He has often stood patiently, listening to me, then said with calm determination, "Maybe I would do it differently. ' And so he made me see what was actually best for me. Especially when I looked back on it.

One of those times was when we decided - it was initially his decision - that I would not participate in the European Championship prior to Sydney. Eddy said I had to build up to the Olympics that took place three months later. To be at my very best, to get in form, I couldn't afford any interruption in the training schedule. I thought that was anything but obvious. I wanted to go. I wanted to be in control. Because, imagine, another Belgian would become European champion and then the Olympic Committee would thendecide to bring that reigning European champion to Sydney instead of me.

But Eddy looked beyond control, to creation. For that European Championship after all, my body would have to suffer again to go back to those 48 kilograms. That takes an immense amount of effort. With the necessary rest before and between matches, and the rest and recovery afterwards, I would have lost four weeks in my preparation for the Games. And wasn't that the bigger goal?

At all times, Eddy remained calm. We chatted about it daily and slowly it dawned on me that a participation in the European Championship was not the best plan, considering the longer term. Eddy was focused and convinced of that all along. But he did not push me on it. He let go of control of the decision and trusted the process. So that I would come to the conclusion that continued training was the way to.

A little story: no other Belgian girl became European champion in the weight class under 48 kg. What happened in Sydney months later is history. My own little history.

Also an entrepreneur who tries to support others as a supportive leader to inspire entrepreneurship, must be able to let go of control. No easy task, because as a born entrepreneur he often still has the microbe to build and create with his own hands. While now he must allow others to create.

The entrepreneur as a supportive leader demonstrates his skills and drive at the service of the other. He sees things before others, because they lack the right experience. And that is often where an issue starts. It requires superhuman control to get people to see what comes naturally to you. You have to allow them to stumble, miss a turn, hit a wall before they do see the light. Of course, you want to save them from pain, but when you deny them those potentially hurtful experiences, you curtail their growth and control their future. Progress is only truly sustainable when you let go of the reins, let go of expectations and control, create the right circumstances and continue to believe in the person. Even if it goes wrong - and it would not if they had followed the advice from the experienced expert, you bite your tongue and keep repeating that you as a leader have every confidence in him or her.

Jef De Wit, the driving force behind the Cronos Group, has built more than five hundred companies. No one I know has that much experience and expertise, and yet he lets go of control and gives young entrepreneurs the space and time to try it themselves. He always stays calm, always makes himself available and approachable, helps people learn from their mistakes, supports them in taking their next step, with many falls and even more times getting up.

Again and again and again. Everyone deserves a chance, a laboratory, a learning process. Control over that is good. But (allowing to) create is better.

Pitfalls for the supportive leader

Empowering others for the greater purpose of their well-being and in the longer term the sustainable well-being of the environment and the ecosystem. Supportive leaders subordinate their own dreams to the dreams of others. They have no expectations, they create the appropriate framework, plant the seed and let the other grow. So much selflessness sounds too good to be true. And sometimes it is. To go from being 'entrepreneurial' to be able to mold into 'supportive' is something a leader sometimes struggles with. Suddenly he becomes almost invisible, has to make do without the applause, he can hardly conceive, create, direct.

So, pitfalls can also arise in the path of the supporting leader. We go through some of the most striking examples.

Only dealing with the right circumstances

This endangers the economic necessity of creation and performance. For example, supportive leadership could lapse into aimless conversations, causing the supportive leader to become indifferent and shrugs off the responsibility - he puts himself offside. But even when a supportive leader is outside the circle, he remains responsible and his role is greater than a mere sounding board.

Ignore yourself in such a way that the higher purpose fades away

A leader can reason and act in such a supportive way, that his goal narrows down to helping others to take steps. In doing so, forgetting that as a supportive leader, he also has a higher goal: the long-term impact on sustainable well-being. As a result, he could end up supporting wrong decisions.

The ego rebels because it does not receive recognition

Sometimes it is very energy-draining to be a supportive leader. A supportive leader also has an ego that needs to be stroked from time to time. But because the focus is on the long term, immediate recognition is rare. This can give rise to frustration, especially in moments where the supportive leader himself is not feeling well.

Not allowing yourself anything dries up your idealism

It could be that a supportive leader is so convinced of his purpose or impact in the long term that he will deny himself everything for this. The well-being of others requires so much attention that he forgets care for himself and insert pit stops. But never allowing yourself anything also cuts into your inherent idealism.

Losing faith in your own knowledge and skills

Just because he is always busy with others, a supportive leader will, in times of uncertainty, wonder what his added value actually is. He runs the risk of getting to a point that he questions his own knowledge and skills. This drains his energy, nutrition that he so desperately needs to be able to properly focus on the supportive leadership. Without full batteries a supportiveleader is lost as he must have energy for himself and others, and his impact in the long term will dissipate.

No more insights into how to live today

Of course, the intention is to be happy today. The supporting leader who only looks into the future threatens to ignore the present. In the long run he no longer knows how to stay with himself in the here and now. Whoever fails to pursue happiness today will also have a harder time finding it tomorrow.

Without expectations you become indifferent

Indeed, the first bond of supportive leadership is "no expectations", but that in no way means that the life path of others leaves you indifferent. On the contrary: supportive leadership is about creating the right conditions so that they can achieve their dreams. Once he succeeds in doing that, it is up to the supportive leader to let go and watch what happens. He must allow self-exploration, and in that respect letting go of expectations towards the other so that they have their own future and can start creating. In this way, a supportive leader continues to watch over himself and his energy, and indifference does not stand a chance.

Together on the way
Inclusive leadership: the seven belts in balance

Switch freely
Balance between 'from within' and 'apart from yourself'
The path to purpose as an art of living
Means progress for people and mankind
We do not leave anyone behind
Together to tomorrowland

The path to purpose as an art of living
Enterprising or supportive, they merge on the path to purpose. Everybody has his unique place, with all its strengths and weaknesses, with all diversity and inefficiency. Not equal, but equivalent. Inclusive.

The path to purpose has neither beginning nor end. The path to 'a tomorrow land', a feasible future, a better world, is never finished. Where inclusive leaders are our guides, alternating between designer (entrepreneurial leadership) and coach (supportive leadership). They provide balance and shift freely between support and entrepreneurship. They are self-aware, forgiving, humane, positive, constructive and creative. Their life's work becomes an art of living.

A tomorrow land is a future towards which we work together, independently of current time, dominant culture or prevailing politics. It is a state of sustainability, where social welfare and economic progress go hand in hand. Where inclusive leaders create the optimal conditions for the self-realization of every human being, backed by technology, innovation and science. Where to participate and doing business is more important than winning.

Technology and science must always serve people, and not the other way around. We are not robots. Our intelligence is not artificial. In any case, it should not be a test of strength, but a relationship of enrichment and complementarity.

In 2020, digitization is global. The boundaries between real and virtual, economy and ecology, life and work blur. Robotization, nanotechnology, 3D printing, the internet of things, biotechnology; the developments follow each other faster and faster. How we produce, consume and interact with each other will change fundamentally. There will be other things that will become important in the years to come as we as a society want to make progress in a sustainable way. That is not a purely economic story. As a society you benefit if the well-being of each person increases, without losing sight that there must be creation, in the hope and expectation that the world will become a place for the generations to come.

Of course, we also welcome economic and technological progress, as long as man is at the center of society. The obsession with economic growth and financial profit seems to have resulted in many losing control of their own destiny. The debate on this needs to be started, beyond the ideological contradictions, beyond populism, beyond polarization.

On the left, people argue for redistribution and solidarity, while the right thinks the free market will solve everything. Balance is desirable: we need entrepreneurial leaders who want to make their dreams come true and convince others to co-create and sell. Likewise, we need supportive leaders who are eliminating themselves and giving others space to pursue their dreams. There are interesting ideas and stands on both ends of the spectrum and good people are ready to put them into practice. But above all, we look forward to inclusive leaders who have realized a long time ago that one is not better than the other. We need both, the entrepreneurs and the supporters, according to the specifics of the circumstances and the characteristics of those involved. Ideally, we learn to switch freely in the moment.

A path is no longer a path along the way
the air no longer air
a home no longer a home.
Only the river knows where it flows.
(Extract from 'GR5', the fiction series by Jan Matthys)

Exploring inclusively

The path to purpose is an art of living that everyone can learn and experience. It does not matter how many people you lead. Whether you run a family, a kindergarten class, a team at the NASA space agency or a company of seven thousand employees. Only our ego prevents us from walking the path to purpose, because that ego mainly wants to win. The path says that entrepreneurship - or taking the next step - is more important than winning.

An inclusive leader does not complain that his employees demand a lot of attention, whereby he does not get his 'operational activities' done. He is there for his people, in all modesty. He thinks of himself, but not in the first place. The path to purpose is very much about trust: trust in your fellow humans is essential and attention to them is necessary. That is contrary to other types of leadership that say trust is good, but control is better.

An inclusive leader is a master of self-awareness and self-acceptance. He knows himself and accepts himself as he is. He sees himself as a toolbox with which he can help others to take steps. That's why he is able to formulate an inspiring vision, with an eye to the future, where winning is not the greatest good. Trying things out, self-exploration, daring to take a step into the unknown leads to wider social progress in the long term. Leaders who take the path to purpose put responsibility where it should be: with those who are willing to take responsibility. This creates connection in an organization. Everyone takes part.

Without these seven aspects it becomes difficult to follow the path to purpose.

Self-awareness. Inclusive leaders dare to show vulnerability in how they really are. They have insight and peace with themselves, so that they radiate an inner peace. They know very well who they are. This allows them to focus one hundred percent on what is being said. The time and security they give to others is mind-blowing.

They are consistent, which means the situation for others is also clear and safe.

Hopeful mindset. Inclusive leaders dare to walk unknown paths, with determination and without fear. They dare to go against established values and principles when necessary.

Forgiving. Inclusive leaders accept the mistakes of others and are not out for revenge. They think it is important that lessons are learned out of those mistakes. Within that framework - the will to learn – much is possible. We are humans, and humans make mistakes. Revenge does not help us on the path to purpose.

On a human scale. Inclusive leaders approach, facilitate and serve others in a tailor-made way. They have the belief that anyone who is good for them in some way, deserves help. Even as a forward-looking leader temporarily on the path of entrepreneurial leadership, he looks carefully at others and their strengths.

Insight into the other. Inclusive leaders are not only getting to know themselves, the insight into the other is at least equally important, if not more important. It sometimes seems to the outside world as if they are inefficient. Inclusive leaders know better: others facilitating their path to self-realization is the basis for social progress.

Forward-looking. Inclusive leaders look to the future, not to control it, but to create it. They embrace whatever comes their way and do not fight against any changes. With respect for the past, inclusive leaders build the future.

Mindful listening. Inclusive leaders listen to understand others, to gain insight (empathic listening). But just as often they are mindful, without anything more, without purpose. They listen because they find it important to be completely there for the other.

'He who is able to keep his balance without being offended, without being disturbed, attains the mastery that one needs in the evolution of life. '

(Inayat Khadas, Native American musician)

Small is great

"Growth is good." It is, but it does not have to be everything. That slogan has also caused things to grow somewhat 'skewed'. The belief that ever-larger structures are more efficient in solving problems is urgently in need of a review. And the free market has turned out a lot less free than we have long thought.

In many sectors, open competition has turned into densification, a de facto monopoly. In IT, for example, all power is in the hands of some giants. Big tech, the six American technology leaders (Alphabet / Google, Amazon, Apple, Facebook, Microsoft, and Netflix), are worth more combined than the 94 companies following them in the top 100.

But mergers and acquisitions in education, the healthcare sector and in government also happen rapidly. Schools, hospitals, residential care centers become mastodons where people are often just a number. From an economic logic, the economies of scale and efficiency gains of this consolidation are self-evident. But such monster structures create distance and take away from commitment and the accessibility. Dealings with each other become colder and more impersonal. People have a much harder time identifying with such a uniform, purely functional environment. Just because something works does not mean it is livable.

Care provider and care recipient, teacher and student, civil servant and citizen, they both benefit from tightening the connection and shortening the 'care lines'. Mutual trust can heal, the feeling of happiness awakens, the well-being of all involved increases noticeably. Numbers are renamed, patients become persons.

At Wingmen we also experiment with entrepreneurship and support on a human scale. We give someone the opportunity to achieve their entrepreneurial dream, based on his or her own strengths. This is how we form a cluster of small-scale, equal companies, each with their own culture. They are managed less from a financial logic, and rather from a human, organic, creative perspective. That can seem very inefficient, but you simply cannot feed projects on a human scale in a one size fits all approach. Our people take steps at their own pace, it is a dance to self-realization. If we zoom out, we also create an inclusive society with people at the center. There is room for everyone, in all diversity. Each person can be themselves and make their unique contribution. Doing business together, creating, helping each other and serving ourselves sustainably of available resources that feel good. With the ultimate goal: to lead a meaningful existence through extracting the best in ourselves and others towards making sustainable progress together. Building big scale through balanced small scale. Local is global. Small becomes great.

For an inclusive society we can draw inspiration from 'society 5.0 'as it is developed in Japan with an eye for economic and social progress, and that in equal measure. The human being is the center of society. Where 'industry 4.0' is still the predominant model in the West, looking at world evolution through a technological, industrial, economic, financial glasses. In society 5.0, the digital and physical space is optimally geared to each other, so that there is a human dimension in which you work and live. Society 5.0 was born in Japan to create the social progress of tomorrow, on the one hand from the opportunities of today (technology), on the other hand with a focus on a society that is as humane as possible.

Regardless of sector or domain, we must safeguard the potential for self-development. As many (preferably all) people as possible should get and seize as many (preferably all) opportunities as possible to experiment, to fail and learn. To be able to do this through exact sciences and technical innovation, we find explanations and solutions for issues that used to seem impossible. The human sciences and the arts provide us insight into ourselves and nurture the creative. The combination of the objective and the subjective, of body and mind, of man and machine, allows us to function better as a team, as an organization and as a society. We understand each other.

On the path to purpose, we push progress fueled by previous generations. It is an art of living that can provide an answer to the challenges of continuous change, uncertainty, and complexity. It can make us stronger and give more confidence in ourselves and in others. It is a positive and hopeful view of the future, also and above all in turbulent times.

"Growth is good." Indeed, when it comes to growth that is both personal and is social. About people who make each other bigger, work and live together. It should not always be about scaling up, profit maximization, and rising stock prices. More important is the quality of life and the social added value. A thriving economy only makes sense if the ecosystem is healthy. Sustainable well-being, that's where the real benefit is long-term. Let's all take a share in that. Because growth is good, progress is better.

Sustainable goals

Dividing the path into milestones, turning a dream into goals. On a global level too, a lot is moving in a favorable direction. The United Nations adopted the *Sustainable Development Goals* at the end of 2015 (SDG), an action plan for the next fifteen years to reduce poverty worldwide and get the planet back into a sustainable orbit. For this, 17 sustainability goals are linked to 169 targets. These goals - which are one and indivisible - reflect the three dimensions of sustainable development: the economic, the social and the ecological aspects.

The SDGs can also be divided into five Ps: *people, planet, prosperity, peace, partnerships.* Because it also needs to remain pleasant, some add "pleasure" to it. So, six Ps.

SDG1 no poverty
SDG2 no hunger
SDG3 good health
SDG1 quality **education**
SDG5 gender equality
SDG6 clean water and sanitation
SDG7 affordable and sustainable energy

SDG8 worthy work and economic growth
SDG9 industry, innovation and infrastructure
SDG10 reduce inequality
SDG11 sustainable cities and communities
SDG12 responsible consumption and production
SDG13 climate action
SDG14 life in the water
SDG15 life on land
SDG16 peace, justice and strong public services
SDG17 partnerships to achieve goals

These goals reconcile two agendas: that of sustainable development and that of development cooperation. The emphasis is on 'universality', which means that its implementation concerns the entire planet, and not just the poorer South. To make the objectives more concrete, 169 targets have been formulated and 242 indicators to measure progress.

It is an approach that combines the best of entrepreneurial and supportive leadership. The UN as inclusive leaders. If international organizations would also increasingly focus on the long term, on well-being of each of us and of the sustainable well-being of the entire world's population, then there is hope. Well-founded hope for genuine globalization that no longer has to take victims.

Ecosystem without egos

Pars pro toto. Each part represents and belongs to a whole. What happens to one human being today is absorbed in the collective history of humanity. Where are we heading together and what role does inclusive leadership play on that long and dangerous journey? That cannot be separated from existential questions such as: 'What is the meaning of life?', 'Does free will exist?', "Where does consciousness come from?" or 'What forms of human organization are possible or desirable? ' Understanding the physical reality, containing human nature, it always remains imperfect. The way you experience reality and get to know people and organizations, determines your path and what an 'inclusive' model can look like, and above all, what you expect to be achieved with that model. Expectation determines future actions.

Liberal humanism has long been the mainstream mindset. It starts from the feelings, emotions and desires of people, and glorifies life. And almost automatically aims to strive for immortality, happiness and divinity. Goals that can only be realized because of what scientists discover and technicians develop.

Liberal humanism, however, is no longer as dominant as it used to be. As the era becomes more digital and the world more virtual, the emergence of robotization and artificial intelligence raises new questions. It is likely that post-humanist developments are on the way, that transcend liberal humanism, and that are not aimed at only improving human conditions but also humans.

At the Cronos Group we integrate both. From the humanist tradition, with respect for the past and a view full of hope for the future inspirer, Jef De Wit shapes that nascent posthumanism through seeing new technology as a reinforcement of the human tissue. An ecosystem in which man and machine are intertwined, nature and technology, software and hardware. An organism, more than an organization.

Progress then proceeds very slowly, often even with an intermediate step backwards. But moving too fast creates counterforces and results in inevitable loss. Likewise, Les Ondes is an exponent of that slow, steady drop-by-drop impact on people's lives and futures. Nothing is mandatory, everything is possible. Moving in a natural setting and still staying on the spot. No illusions and yet progress. Not changed and yet touched. The individual action is just as superfluous as the proverbial wing beat of the butterfly, but that one wing beat can take the future form. The hope and expectation are well-founded.

Where entrepreneurial leadership defines itself as 'creating from yourself to realize your ambition', supportive leadership aims for raising awareness, holistically focused on the other, the environment, on the entire ecosystem. The inclusive leader can switch between entrepreneurial and supportive, between 'hard' and 'soft'. Everything to guarantee the evolutionary process of the ecosystem. Consider an inclusive leader leadership as a spectrum in which there is no room for personal gain. After all, the ecosystem has only one goal: survival.

A soft leader is a master in dealing with (in)visibility. In and out of the action. Like a mental trapeze worker, he balances on a tightrope. Step by step, without expectation of reaching the end point, because there is none. The line is a loop, a cycle. On the way is the way.

There are milestones, but after every step the world can look a little different. It is all so fragile that grand goals do not make sense. It is about survival on the tightrope. You can dream, but not too much. An inclusive leader must judge in the here and now, knowing what each step can mean for the future. An inclusive leader is mindful listener who is not guided by emotions. He defuses situations and lightens the burden by probing what someone really needs, beyond the emotions.

To change the world, you have to be patient, not preoccupied with judging, not pursuing personal success. It is a bigger mission, to make a group of people look at themselves and their environment differently and draw strength from that. Of course, money is nice, and yes, you earn more if you work efficiently. In that regard, entrepreneurial leaders often perform better - in hard numbers anyway - then supportive leaders. But supportive and inclusive leaders create the conditions in which to be entrepreneurial leaders can work. This keeps the engine running.

Complexity, inefficiency and diversity do not have to weigh on the survival of the ecosystem. On the contrary, we live with people who think, speak, behave differently. Efficiency is not a natural habitat. It is 'cultivated' behavior. The jungle is the purest form of an ecosystem, all complexity and diversity, but no efficiency. Survival is the only gain. That is in contrast to a banana plantation where there is no room for complexity, diversity and individual input. Everything is done according to standard procedures and that brings in a lot of money. But the first banana grows in the wild before it can be 'tamed'. The plantation does not exist without the jungle.

The Cronos Group is also an ecosystem aimed at its own survival. The evolutionary process is the goal, without pressure, without expectations. Without permanent control too. A central platform only serves as support of people who want to take the next step. Which step and what kind of help they want from the central platform; they decide for themselves. Sometimes quality suffers because of the diversity and complexity. That is okay. Everyone does it their own way, on their own. As long as the quality loss does not cause irreparable damage to the ecosystem.

Three quarters of the hundred new companies do not work, but at least it has been tried. The Cronos Group is driven by diversity and

complexity. There is room for everyone to have their place within the ecosystem. The companies form tribes. People find each other when they need to. This does not have to be organized in a formal way. The Cronos Group wants to give young people the opportunity to build something. Someone who comes with the intention of offering something to the group is pointless. The ecosystem will sustain itself. It will itself indicate what needs to be done. Entrepreneurial leaders can also thrive and grow within the ecosystem,
but then organically and with patience.

As a result

The guide in you

One day I wanted to be the best in the world. Now I want all the best for the world. Of course, I do not have the wisdom, that is not what this book wishes to pretend. It is not based on scientific research or theoretical study. It does not proclaim truth and does not preach morals. It is neither law nor commandment. It does not provide a formula for success. You cannot take it to the stock exchange.

For me it is more like a travel journal, a collection of experiences, insights and conversations that I encountered on my path during and after sports. Curiosity about myself and about others are my compass. What I hope is that the path to purpose can serve as an inspiration for anyone who wants to take a step forward on the path to self-realization. As I have done and will continue to do, through trial and error, supporting and being supportive of others.

As a former judoka I had to reinvent myself. Or rather: looking for what was left of me after the last applause died out. The pilot flame beyond the Olympic fire. After a professional sports career you tumble into a black hole. But you can climb out of that and again be the light. With more clarity than before. Loud and clear. It takes courage to go for a new life. But the enrichment is greater than medals or money. The realization of being a part of the world, as a person between the people, the confidence to make a difference, however small, and being able to turn dreams into goals and actions.

Today I coach young entrepreneurs, I let others excel. I never thought that standing behind the scenes - or next to the stage - would be so satisfying. Rest assured: if I walk or bike after hours, I still want to be the fastest, but the world does not necessarily need to know that. Now you know.

As mentioned, this is not a traditional manager's story or a manual with models and charts. But it is also not a homeopathic dilution or noncommittal vagueness. The path to purpose is not for softies. It wants to get rid of the machismo that has characterized capitalism for so long, where it is still 'hard above heart'. Even on Wall Street they are gradually pretending to realize that things have to be done differently. And if they pretend long enough, it will be that way. Whatever that difference will look like, I look forward to it with you. But instead of passively waiting for it, we can take responsibility, grab the handlebars, direct yourself and go a long way down that path.

A softer road therefore, an art of living, as a balance between different types of leadership. In this way we can improve the cultural, economic, technological, and social challenges we stand for, in a different way and progress from the past in a respectful manner and take it positively into an inclusive future.

The absolute model of leadership does not exist. No more than I believe anyone can be approached in the same way when taking another step. The many views and theories of leadership that I read just taught me that every vision has its value, every theory has its value, it deserves to be put into practice. A specific form of leadership is a crossroads on a spectrum. There are authoritarian leaders, there are predominantly servant leaders, there are resolutely enterpreneurial leaders, there are so-called quantum leaders. But there is only one leader like yourself. Leadership is tailor-made.

I have come to that insight, one of many, thanks to and often together with my partner Wim. I want to explicitly thank him here, for testing ideas, weighing up words, finishing each other's sentences.

And of course, I would also like to thank Jef De Wit, the driving force behind the Cronos Group and my guide on the path to purpose. He made me see an ecosystem is so much greater than any ego. That we can never leave anyone behind. Entrepreneurship and support, following and leading are all part of the same cycle. That anyone can become a guide in their own path to purpose. Hopefully you also feel addressed.

To tomorrowland
Letter from Jef De Wit

When we met Ann in October 2013, I did not immediately expect to get hold of a book of hers years later, wherein the Cronos Group and myself are presented so positively. But that is Ann: when she goes for something, she is all in, with heart and soul. That can also be felt clearly in this experienced and thoughtful story. I am happy to have been able to make a small contribution.

Dirk Deroost and I set up the Cronos Group as a platform to give talented young people the opportunity to grow personally and, if desired, boost their professional career, up to and including entrepreneurship. At our first contact, Ann was looking for meaning. She was ready for a 'trip to her tomorrowland' and found the ideal ecosystem to take risks in complete safety with us. The framework we provide for our 'entrepreneurs' is one at elite sport level. The Olympic idea is never far away here: entrepreneurship is more important than winning. We unburden, guide and challenge when necessary. With a lot of freedom to choose their own path, to be able to make mistakes and learn from it.

After her sports career, Ann connected with us quickly and organically, she familiarized herself with the model. Meanwhile, she has guided many people with talent, enthusiasm and common sense to the next step. That guidance can be done in every possible and impossible place. At the Cronos Group we do indeed have our own own 'path to purpose' to a place that can be shared with others. Not too far and yet remote enough. Clear and yet a bit invisible. An idea was given an address and the dream a name, Les Ondes. More than fifteen thousand people have already found their way there. Among them many potential entrepreneurs, of the hard and soft type, headstrong or inclusive. Whoever has been there continues the tradition and comes back with his or her own team. Drops become rivers, to the rhythm of Les Ondes - the waves.

When we sincerely listen and think sustainably ahead, the future shines through the trees. A 'tomorrow' that is built on enlightenment ideals of reason, science and technology, humanism and progress. A 'tomorrow' where experience, knowledge and skills are passed on to the next generations.

We wish everyone the right way. It can be a long road full of danger, but together we are stronger, smarter and more inventive. On to the future, our tomorrow land, an inclusive society. With experienced guides like Ann.

We do not leave anyone behind.

Regards
Jef

Overview

The tires of the path to purpose

Entrepreneurial leadership
1. Take responsibility
2. Become the architect of your own life
3. A goal is a dream with a deadline
4. Take control of the wheel

Supportive leadership
5. No expectations
6. Create the framework
7. Plant the seed

Inclusive leadership

The 7 belts in balance

Characteristics of an entrepreneurial leader
How do entrepreneurial leaders act?

• In action
An entrepreneurial leader takes action himself in the physical world. He is a doer, does not give up and places himself centrally, in the focal point of the action.

• Visible
An entrepreneurial leader is visible to his team and to the outside world. He is the face of what he wants to create and takes responsibility for it. He wants to work with a team to create, sell (convince) and deliver.

• From within
An enterpreneurial leader creates from within himself. He knows himself quite well. He knows he is responsible for his own life, he wants to be the director of it, make his dreams come true, and he is extremely aware of his own strengths. He also realizes that he needs to pay attention for the dreams, goals and strengths of his environment (team, competition, business

partner, life partner), to increase his chances of success (realizing its goals).

Steps forward
- by making mistakes.
- evaluate what could be improved.
- apply that.
- continue.

Dealing with innovation
Develop the probability directions yourself and try out the ideas with a team. (A probability direction is one direction the team can go in.) Naturally, the entrepreneurial leader thinks up his own probability direction and likes to try new things himself. He is in fact working from within himself on his dream. That is what typifies the enterpreneurial leader. He is not afraid to ask for help in fine-tuning his probability directions. An entrepreneurial leader does not mind being challenged and listens to how others see the world. He accepts the help, but his proactivity leaves him the responsibility to determine the path.

Time perception

Every day an entrepreneur focuses on:

- the short term.
- the medium term.

In his daily tasks he is busy with tactics. So, on the one hand, he is busy with plans how to implement strategic vision and goals within the short or medium term (in most cases over a maximum of one year). On the other hand, he often does operational duties himself. He often assists in the process of finding a solution to deliver to the customer. These are the tasks of the entrepreneurial leader in the here and now.

Growth rate

That is determined by the entrepreneurial leader and his team. If the enterprising leader and his team no longer have the energy to tell the story, there is a problem. When the dream is no longer carried out by the entrepreneurial leader and his team, the growth rate comes to a standstill.

Behavioral focus

An entrepreneurial leader focuses on:

- effectiveness: an entrepreneurial leader wonders every day whether he is doing the right things.
- efficiency: efficiency is about doing things right. You do things right and purposefully.

You may be able to pick pears very efficiently, but if you prefer to eat cherries, you are not doing things effectively.

Target

An enterprising leader advances rapidly if he can convert dreams into concrete SMART goals.

S pecific: an objective should not be too general. It must deal with something specific.

M easurable: you have to be able to count, measure or tick off an objective. By December 31 next year I want to hire **five** newly graduated IT staff. Five is measurable.

A ttainable: are the goals attainable for the target group and the management? Do you not exhaust your team too much with the objective? Does your team have the necessary strengths to bear the objectives? Are the objectives consistent with the objectives of the management, of the external shareholders or the wider environment?

R ealistic: is the goal achievable? Is it feasible in terms of both budget and relative to the ins and outs of the market, the fluctuation of supply and demand, to hire five recently graduated IT staff?

T ime-bound: at what date in the calendar must the goal be reached?

By December 31 next year I want to hire five IT graduates. Which is a very clear point in time: the last day of the coming year.

Fight

An enterprising leader is convinced that he has to fight. He has to beat his competitors. Make a profit. But not for any price, nor at all costs, see next point.

Dealing with the environment

• An entrepreneurial leader strives for a **win-win**. He is fully aware that he must also motivate the people around him to follow his dream. In that respect, he not only wants to write the success story himself, but that his team contributes to the success story.

- Listening empathetically. Listening to learn instead of listening to answer.

Characteristics of a supportive leader

How do supportive leaders act?

• Outside the action
Supportive leaders do not create things themselves. They support or guide others. They move outside the circle and support others to make their dreams come true.

• Invisible
Supportive leaders are quite invisible to the outside world. They are obviously visible to those who they help but remain in the shadows. Supportive leaders are certainly not the face of a team or of a project. From the relative shelter they strive for sustainable well-being of their environment.

• Independent of itself
Supportive leaders do not create. They know themselves very well and can subordinate their own dreams to the dreams of entrepreneurial people leaders or others. For this they have to break free from themselves and be able to view

everything from a distance. They know they are responsible for their own lives. Yet they mainly want to create the right conditions so that others can create, supply and sell, for a higher long-term goal.

Steps forward
• by experiencing what it is like to facilitate others independently of yourself;
• to sense where things can be improved;
• support from there.

Dealing with innovation
Supportive leaders provide tools and resources with which others can come up with their own opportunities and thus make their dream come true. Supporting leaders therefore do not come up with opportunities themselves. Supportive leaders make their know-how available. They facilitate, motivating and pampering with the aim of increasing the individual well-being of others. The overarching mission is the sustainable well-being of society. Innovation can lead to change. Innovation as inspiration.

Time perception

Supporting leaders focus daily on:

• the long term;

• the very long term.

Of course, supportive leaders also live in the present. The daily things must happen in the here and now. But because they facilitate others separate from themselves, they do things with an impact on the long-term or even very long-term. A supportive leader who is aware of this is not easily scared off or discouraged by short-term setbacks. Only if things happen today that serve the higher purpose - the sustainable well-being of the environment or the ecosystem - he will respond himself.

Growth rate

Supportive leaders do not push a pace like entrepreneurial leaders tend to do but bring others into sync with their own rhythm. They allow them to feel and track their heartbeat. The basis for natural growth.

Behavioral focus

Supportive leaders focus on **complexity and diversity**. They allow for complexity and diversity without frustration, because they increase the opportunity for self-realization for everyone. Ultimately, this leads to sustainable well-being for the environment or the ecosystem. Everyone is different and can live according to his or her own path. Self-determination, self-reliance and self-development (together: self-realization), individual well-being and sustainable well-being thrive on an approach on a human scale.

Target
Supportive leaders aim at the well-being of society with a long-term vision, based on love and a sense of responsibility for the world (or at least the environment around them). You can see that as an evolutionary target. The concrete milestones along the way evolve over time. The bottom line is that supportive leaders want long-term impact with sustainable well-being and progress as a leading motive.

Fight

Unlike entrepreneurial leaders, supportive leaders do not fight. Because they understand the art of serving a higher purpose is acting independently of themselves, they can easily defuse and transcend conflict. They look, feel, evaluate and anticipate. " Peace Love Unity Respect " is not a hollow slogan for them.

Dealing with the environment
• Supportive leaders always share.
• They plant the seed of knowledge and skills.
• They make resources available.
• They listen mindfully. That's one step further than empathetic listening, what aims to understand the other. Mindful listening to someone is to be there for him. Nothing more, nothing less.

Ann thanks

'Rien n'est plus fort qu'une idée dont l'heure est venue', wrote Victor Hugo - there is nothing more powerful than an idea whose time has come.

Jef De Wit, our CEO, must have thought that when he came back in November 2018 and planted the seed: writing a book about how I view the world, maybe that could be the next project. Without further expectation, he walked on. My first thanks go to him - much more than our CEO, he is a constant source of inspiration. What a privilege this has been. The search for the right approach started that Monday in November 2018.

The result, the book you are holding, is a message about the path of self-realization and the role that leadership plays in it. Looking for the right words I had countless conversations with people who constantly challenged my ideas. I am extremely grateful for these conversations, for anyone who has been patient with me for the past 40 years and supported me in making my dream come true.

Special thanks go to my *Wingmen* : Martijn, Lennert, Ward and Mathias from Headr, Tim from Potvos, Tim, Stefan and Isabeau from Fueled and Marlies from Untranslate. We are building Wingmen together and I am lucky to get to work with such strong, young, passionate people. While writing, I may have not been available enough for them. They were always there for me.

Also to my publisher Niels, who kept me on track. With respect for what was already there, but also with a loving reference to the work still to do. To Lotte who took care of a wonderful coordination, to Tim who helped me to market the book, to Peer who designed the layout and to Johan Faes. I was lucky that Johan wanted to my editor. He is one of the best in the business. Every time I stand amazed how he transforms my half sentences into a logical whole. Into a text that says exactly what I want to say.

To the BOIC and the Judo federation, especially Eddy and Jean-Marie. To my club coaches Frits, Hugo and Jean-Jacques. We won that Olympic medal together.

Here I also get the chance to do what I have done far too little: to thank my parents and my sister. They have sacrificed a large part of their lives for my judo dream. Then I did not realize that yet, but they were the greatest supportive leaders I've known. I owe them a lot.

Finally, I would like to thank my friend Wim and my son Ruben. Wim, days and nights we talked about what message I wanted to convey. You read books about it yourself. Our last vacation in Tuscany was all about the path to purpose. Even at New Year, in the Tuscan sun, I was writing down ideas. You looked at me, supported me and waited until I had a moment to go have an Italian coffee. Dear Wim, it has not always been easy in recent years. You did not know what to do with my fickleness, but you always followed the path to purpose. Thank you for this.

Ruben, you have been my mirror for ten years. Because you are who you are – sometimes opposite to me - you teach me so much. You live in amazement for the world around you. You are also very enthusiastic and proud of the path to purpose. While you secretly realize that I have been doing this for the past few months and had less time for you. If you later read this book and are a daddy yourself, you will realize that you have contributed greatly to it. 'You are just the way you are,' said Miss Eva, and she's right. I hope I can provide you lasting support and confidence no matter what.

www.ingramcontent.com/pod-product-compliance
Lightning Source LLC
Chambersburg PA
CBHW070538220526
45467CB00003B/990